The SWIMMING HOLES OF Texas

NUMBER FORTY-FOUR
Jack and Doris Smothers Series in
Texas History, Life, and Culture

Updated Edition

The SWIMMING HOLES OF *Texas*

JULIE WERNERSBACH & CAROLYN TRACY

Photography by
CAROLYN TRACY

UNIVERSITY OF TEXAS PRESS ᐯ AUSTIN

Publication of this work was made possible in part by support from the J. E. Smothers, Sr., Memorial Foundation and the National Endowment for the Humanities.

Requests for permission to reproduce material from this work should be sent to:

> Permissions
> University of Texas Press
> P.O. Box 7819
> Austin, TX 78713-7819
> utpress.utexas.edu/rp-form

♾ The paper used in this book meets the minimum requirements of ANSI/NISO Z39.48-1992 (R1997) (Permanence of Paper).

LIBRARY OF CONGRESS CATALOGING-IN-PUBLICATION DATA

Names: Wernersbach, Julie, author. | Tracy, Carolyn, author, photographer.
Title: The swimming holes of Texas / Julie Wernersbach and Carolyn Tracy ; photography by Carolyn Tracy.
Description: Updated edition. | Austin : University of Texas Press, 2020 | First edition, 2017.
    Identifiers: LCCN 2016037835
    ISBN 978-1-4773-2152-2 (pbk. : alk. paper)
    ISBN 978-1-4773-2153-9 (library e-book)
    ISBN 978-1-4773-2154-6 (nonlibrary e-book)
Subjects: LCSH: Texas—Guidebooks. | Swimming—Texas—Guidebooks. | Outdoor recreation—Texas—Guidebooks. | Recreation areas—Texas—Guidebooks.
Classification: LCC F384.3 .T73 2017 | DDC 917.640464—dc23
LC record available at https://lccn.loc.gov/2016037835

doi:10.7560/321522

Contents

Introduction

SWIM THE LONE STAR STATE

It's the middle of July. Bank marquees and car thermometers clock another 104° day. Air conditioners moan. Brooklyn transplants weep. Everyone sweats. Across Texas, drivers gingerly pull seat belts across our laps, careful to avoid meeting skin to scorching metal. We settle Topo Chicos into cup holders, crank as much cold air as our car engines can summon, and point our vehicles toward the only destination that holds relief: one of Texas's natural swimming holes.

As quintessential to Texas as Lone Star Beer, barbecue, and Willie Nelson's Fourth of July picnic, swimming holes are vital to surviving the region's endless, sweltering summers. Ordinary concrete pools don't compare to the transcendent calm of clear springwater, old-growth trees, and wide-open skies; they can't offer the sense of adventure that comes from piling friends, family, and picnic essentials in the car for a road trip, short or long.

But how do you choose which of the dozens of possible oases to visit? Pedernales Falls? Blue Hole? Garner State Park? Amistad Reservoir? Boykin Springs? The state of Texas is home to hundreds of lakes, rivers, and spring-fed holes, each one boasting its own unique natural magic. Otherworldly grottoes and waterfalls, hidden canyons, and an endless variety of animal and plant life distinguish each sweet spot from the next one on the map. Where do you begin?

This guide is here to help. *The Swimming Holes of Texas* is a curated list of over one hundred of the best swim spots across the state. From as far north as Quanah to as far west as Balmorhea, these are top recommended places to jump into natural water and cool off, based on empirical research conducted by two authors armed with towels, sunscreen, and the mission to drive across Texas tracking down every promising piece of water on the map. The guiding criteria were simple: Is this water we want to swim in? Are there reasonable amenities? Do we feel safe and relaxed? And, most important, would we want to come here again?

Preserved, protected, and sources of pride, the swimming holes of Texas and the parks that house them are among the Lone Star State's most celebrated pleasures. Keep this guide in your bag or backseat all summer long as inspiration for spontaneous road trips and weekend adventures. With this book in one hand and a bottle of sunblock in the other, you'll be ready to dive into everything a Texas summer has to offer.

Planning Your Trip

This guide is organized around six regions: North, East, Central, Austin and surrounding area, South, and West. We define North as the area north of Georgetown, including the Dallas–Fort Worth metroplex and the Panhandle. East includes the Pineywoods and Big Thicket regions. South encompasses locales south of Interstate 10 and east of I-35. West covers anything that lies west of Utopia and south of I-10.

Basic information regarding operating hours, fees, amenities, and park rules is included. For comprehensive and up-to-the-minute information, call ahead to your destination or visit its website.

Fees listed pertain to day use only. Additional fees are typically required for camping, boating, and other activities. Hours listed refer to day-use areas. Office hours vary.

For the purposes of this guide, information focuses on the swim experience at each location. Often, particularly in the case of state parks, these destinations have plenty more to offer, including extensive hiking trails, guided tours, camping, and additional recreational activities. Take time to get to know a place, either by stopping at a visitors' center when you arrive or checking its website in advance. May the promise of swimming lure you into unexpected adventures on your trip!

Natural swimming holes are, above all else, ruled by one power: Mother Nature. Water levels and swim experiences will vary depending on weather, annual rainfall, and other environmental factors. Swimming areas within designated parks may be closed because of environmental conditions like drought, flooding, or contamination. Because posted conditions may be unavailable and can rapidly change, careful consideration must be applied when enjoying a swimming hole. Always avoid swimming in stagnant water, drinking untreated water, and fully submerging oneself if there is cause for concern. Texas Parks & Wildlife is diligent about updating the status of its parks and water areas on each state park's web page. The best way to know what to expect at a destination, however, is to call ahead.

Texas is known for its heat and its swimming. It's not known for its abundant shade. Potable water is not always available at a swim spot, especially if it's all natural and undeveloped. Bring more water with you than you think you'll need. Sunscreen and general sun protection are highly recommended.

Packing list: Sunscreen. Sunhat. Towel. Water shoes (or hiking boots, depending on the terrain). Drinking water. Trash bag.

Pro tip: For the state parks listed in this guide, the searchable Texas Parks & Wildlife website (tpwd.texas.gov/state-parks) provides invaluable information, including printable PDFs of park maps, written driving directions, and GPS coordinates.

Swimmers' Etiquette

Clean up after yourself. Pollution from human trash threatens the vitality and beauty of these places we hold so dear. If you carried it in, carry it back out. If your pet left it behind, clean it up before you go. Pet waste is a serious source of water pollution.

Leave every piece of the park behind. Artifacts, animals, stones, and every bit of the environment you visit is protected and must remain where you discovered it. Take a photo, not the object.

Obey all posted park rules. They exist for the preservation and protection of the natural environment and for your safety.

Stay on designated trails. Every step we take impacts the natural world. Many of the state's natural areas have undergone—or are in the process of—rehabilitation. Keeping to designated trails ensures that ecological environments in Texas continue to have every opportunity to thrive. Also keep in mind that poisonous plants can live in the uncultivated parts of parks.

If a sign says "No Diving," don't dive. Often what looks like a deep river or lake hides boulders and other unseen, fatal dangers at its bottom. Stay safe and swim as designated.

Respect your fellow swimmers. The water in Texas belongs to everyone. Be respectful when launching your tubes, your inflatable canoes, and yourself into the water. Pick up after yourself and your pets to keep the water and park clean for your fellow swimmers.

Consider what you really need to enjoy the space. Will those extra six butterfly chairs really make the difference between a good time and a day you'll never forget? Is the terrain you're visiting amenable to pop-up tents and coolers the size of refrigerators?

Keep young swimmers safe. Life vests and reliable floatation devices are recommended for young swimmers. Be mindful of river currents and varying depths in lakes. Never leave children unattended in the water.

History and Conservation

Follow US Highway 90 forty miles west of Del Rio in the lower Pecos region of Texas, and you'll find a four-thousand-year-old painting on a rock wall, one of the most photographed pictographs in the area. Located in what is now the Galloway White Shaman Preserve, the image is attributed to prehistoric inhabitants of the area. It's believed that within this pictograph lies what very well may be the first cartographic depiction of Texas: a map of the springs of the Edwards Aquifer, including Barton and San Marcos Springs. Each year guided tours bring visitors down into the canyon to observe this remarkable link in the chain of human history—our shared experience of the same water sources.

Long before we had cars to get us there, before the missionaries arrived, before settlers built tourist destinations and began to document springs in advertisements and deeds, before the native tribes traded with and defended against the settlers and missionaries—even before someone lifted a hand to a cave wall to record what had been seen—human beings sought the rivers, springs, and lakes in Texas for renewal, survival, and spiritual strength. When you visit these sites, you're participating in a story that is thousands of years old. Continuing our intrinsic relationship with these waterways is a significant responsibility.

To pass along this sacred story of water and land to our children and their descendants, we must preserve and protect these resources today. Population growth and development across Texas have strained aquifers that once supported artesian springs that spouted ten feet into the air and have threatened the quality of crystal-clear rivers. As more and more people draw from the same water sources, how we treat these resources is vital to our future.

Water conservation begins at home with mindfulness of how long and often we run our faucets, whether or not we water our lawns, and how we wash our cars. Conservation is with us on our neighborhood streets as we clear litter out of storm drains and consider the effects that pesticides and household chemicals have on the bodies of water our sewage systems and drainage pipes eventually dump into. And, of course, conservation is most obviously with us when we visit natural treasures and take care to keep our beloved waters and their surrounding lands as we discovered them—clean of human trash and debris, each stone, leaf, and feather left where we found it.

Appreciating the swim experiences outlined in this book means being a good and faithful steward of the resources that sustain and connect us across human history. Protect them today so that we can continue to share them tomorrow.

Park Rules and Regulations

Texas boasts an extensive, well-maintained state park system. From the Panhandle to the Gulf Coast, Texas Parks & Wildlife provides high quality, comfortable places for individuals and families to camp, hike, and connect with the natural world.

The state's extensive park system began with the work of the Civilian Conservation Corps (CCC) in the 1930s and '40s. As part of Franklin Roosevelt's New Deal legislation to create jobs during the Great Depression, crews of young men were tasked with developing state and national parks across the country. The members of the CCC in Texas spent years building dams, bathhouses, pavilions, roads, picnic benches, and much more, forging parks out of each location's native materials. A portion of each worker's paycheck was sent back home to his family, as was an annual newsletter that updated family members on the educational, spiritual, and recreational lives of the men.

The work of the CCC is on brilliant display in twenty-nine state parks across Texas. The craftsmanship and attention to detail testify to the pride taken in this work. Their efforts are well documented and often are described on plaques and exhibits at the parks. Take time to appreciate their enduring work and pick up a copy of *The Civilian Conservation Corps in Texas State Parks* if you see it at a park store.

TEXAS STATE PARK RULES AND REGULATIONS

For a full list of Texas state park rules and regulations, visit the Texas Parks & Wildlife website (tpwd.texas.gov). Included here are a few general rules for visitors to keep in mind.

Swimming must occur only in areas open for swimming. Night swimming is not allowed unless otherwise posted.

Glass containers are not permitted in the water or in the beach area adjacent to the water.

Pets are not allowed inside buildings or in designated swim areas. Pets are permitted in parks but must remain on leash.

Nudity is not permitted.

Alcohol consumption, the display of open containers in public, and the sale of alcohol are prohibited.

Plants and wildlife are protected. It is an offense to mutilate, destroy, or remove plant life. It is an offense to harm, harass, disturb, trap, confine, feed, or remove any wildlife. Bird feeding may be permitted on a park-by-park basis.

Geological and cultural features and artifacts are protected. It is an offense to remove, destroy, deface, or tamper with any rock, earth, soil, gem, mineral, fossil, geological deposit, artifact, or cultural feature.

NATIONAL PARK RULES AND REGULATIONS

For a full list of national park rules and regulations, visit the National Park Service website (nps.gov). Included here are a few general rules for visitors to observe.

Pets must remain on leash at all times. Pets are not permitted in swimming areas or sanitary facilities.

Leave natural areas the way you find them. Preserve and protect your national forests, national parks, and Army Corps of Engineers lake areas. Do not carve, chop, cut, or damage any live trees.

Clean up after yourself and your pets. Help prevent pollution by keeping garbage, litter, and foreign substances out of lakes, streams, and other waters.

The
SWIMMING
HOLES
OF
Texas

North

North Texas, defined here as a broad swath north of Georgetown—including the Dallas–Fort Worth area, Lubbock, and the Panhandle—is a region rich in lake life. Up here, you'll find flat prairie grasslands butting up against the spectacular red-rock views of the Caprock escarpment. Wind turbines spin like friendly giants and long country roads take you from Dinosaur Valley to Lake Brownwood to Possum Kingdom. Head east and you'll find several river headwaters, including the Trinity, whose four branches have been dammed to form many terrific swimming lakes, including Ray Roberts and Lewisville Lakes. Keep an eye out for prairie dogs in these parts and be mindful that up north, Texas really does get to know a good winter freeze. Make sure you get your swim in while the sun is high and the air is warm.

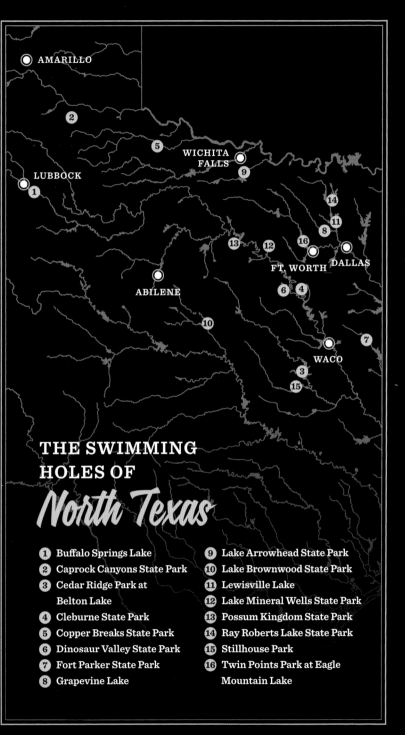

THE SWIMMING HOLES OF
North Texas

1. Buffalo Springs Lake
2. Caprock Canyons State Park
3. Cedar Ridge Park at Belton Lake
4. Cleburne State Park
5. Copper Breaks State Park
6. Dinosaur Valley State Park
7. Fort Parker State Park
8. Grapevine Lake
9. Lake Arrowhead State Park
10. Lake Brownwood State Park
11. Lewisville Lake
12. Lake Mineral Wells State Park
13. Possum Kingdom State Park
14. Ray Roberts Lake State Park
15. Stillhouse Park
16. Twin Points Park at Eagle Mountain Lake

Buffalo Springs Lake

9999 High Meadow Road
Lubbock, TX 79404
(806) 747-3353
buffalospringslake.net

HOURS: Gate is open 24/7.

ENTRANCE FEES: $11 per adult. $5 ages 6–11. Free ages 5 and under. $6 for active military members and seniors 65 and older. Additional fees apply for watercraft, dirt bikes, ATVs, and camping. An additional $1 processing fee is charged for all credit and debit card transactions.

PARK RULES: Glass containers and littering prohibited.

CAMPING: Primitive, tent, and RV (water and electric hookups). Waterfront camping available. Campgrounds do become crowded during the busy summer season.

ABOUT: Located fifteen to twenty minutes east of Lubbock, Buffalo Springs is a gated residential village that offers opportunities for swimming, boating, and camping to nonresidents. Visitors pay an entrance fee that permits access to Buffalo Springs Lake, hiking trails, and all other outdoor amenities. The lake community is notable for being set in Yellow House Draw, a canyon that cuts through the Caprock escarpment. While the cliffs aren't as tall or pronounced as in other areas of northeast Texas, swimming in Buffalo Springs Lake still affords you views of some of that transporting red caliche. Although a dam has inundated the springs, they still flow beneath the surface of the lake.

SWIMMING: There are two man-made beaches at Buffalo Springs, both with roped-off swim areas that drop off steeply. Both shorelines are packed with a thick layer of red sand, reminiscent of the vibrant color of the surrounding red rocks of the Caprock escarpment. The first beach you'll come upon after entering the village is Marina Beach on Pony Express Trail. This long, narrow swim spot is conveniently located and easy to find. The second, Sandy Point, is in a more spacious cove a bit farther away. Take the asphalt bridge over the lake to find this spot where a grass lawn slopes down to meet the sand, offering more space to post up. No lifeguards are on duty at either beach; swim at your own risk. Be sure young swimmers use life jackets or floatation devices.

AMENITIES: Restrooms. Pavilion available for rent.

PRO TIP: Be sure to swing through Lubbock, home of rock-and-roll legend Buddy Holly. Check out the Buddy Holly Center, where you can watch a short film about his life and see a variety of memorabilia, including the famous pair of frame glasses the musician was wearing in his final moments.

Caprock Canyons State Park

PO Box 204
Quitaque, TX 79255
(806) 455-1492
tpwd.texas.gov/state-parks/caprock-canyons

HOURS: 8 a.m.–5 p.m.

ENTRANCE FEES: $5 per adult. Free ages 12 and under. Camping fees apply.

PARK RULES: Texas Parks & Wildlife rules apply.

CAMPING: Primitive, tent, equestrian, and RV (water and electric hookups).

ABOUT: Who needs the Grand Canyon? That's what you may ask yourself not long after driving into Caprock Canyons State Park. Located in the Texas Panhandle on FM 1065, three and a half miles north of State Highway 86 in Quitaque, the park offers phenomenal views of the Caprock escarpment in northeast Texas: pink rolling hills, red-orange cliff faces, and the sort of sweeping landscape you might expect to find hours farther west. The metal bison that adorn the grounds near the visitors' center indicate the park's unique mission as a preservation range for the Texas State Bison Herd, the last of the great southern plains bison. Rangers actively work to conserve the herd by expanding its territory into the park's hundred thousand acres. If you ask a ranger the last place the herd was seen roaming, you'll hear they're often found near campgrounds and in public areas of the park. (There are some basic bison safety precautions to be aware of, so be sure to get yourself up to speed in the visitors' center. Remember, by Texas state law it's a class C Parks and Wildlife Code misdemeanor to feed or offer food to any wildlife in a state park.) Thirteen trails wind through the park, with individual parking lots at trailheads accessible outside the park's main entrance. Some of these trails cover serious, rough terrain. Climb bluffs and cliffs at your own risk. Mountain biking, camping, and boating are also popular here.

SWIMMING: Lake Theo, created by a dam on Holmes Creek, offers an easy spot to cool off at Caprock. Take the road across from the Honea Flat camping area all the way down to a parking area at the top of a steep grass hill dotted with covered picnic tables and shade trees. This grassy bank curls around the water to create a cove where access to the roped-off swim area is as simple as walking into the water. The lake bottom is soft and spotted with vegetation. Squeamish steppers will want to wear swim shoes. No lifeguard is on duty; swim at your own risk.

AMENITIES: Restrooms with showers. Picnic tables with grills. Playground. Amphitheater. Boat ramp. Scenic overlooks galore.

PRO TIP: Take a side trip out of Quitaque to nearby Turkey, Texas, onetime home of country legend Bob Wills and site of the annual "Bob Wills Day."

Cedar Ridge Park at Belton Lake

3790 Cedar Ridge Park Road
Temple, TX 76502
(254) 986-1404
swf-wc.usace.army.mil/belton

HOURS: 6 a.m.–10 p.m.

ENTRANCE FEES: Free. Camping fees apply.

PARK RULES: Glass containers and firearms prohibited. Pets must be on leash. Army Corps of Engineers rules of use apply. Obey all posted rules.

CAMPING: Tent, RV (water and electric hookups), and screened shelters.

ABOUT: In the Brazos River basin just west of Temple, midway between Austin and Waco and close to the Fort Hood army base, an impounded portion of the Leon River serves as a reservoir, fish and wildlife habitat, and recreational lake. Belton Lake was formed in 1954 when the Army Corps of Engineers completed a dam that would provide flood control and utilize the river for Belton, Temple, and other nearby towns. Boat ramps, camping, swim beaches, and more make the 136 miles of shoreline surrounding this 12,300-acre lake a popular destination. Rocky cliffs and limestone bluffs around the lake provide great scenic spots for picnicking and taking in the view. Visitors in late spring and early summer may notice a sulfur smell to the lake, as it naturally "turns over," shifting layers of water from top to bottom and releasing hydrogen sulfide gas in the process. The lake's

designated swim beaches have been significantly affected by flooding from heavy rain in 2016. Cedar Ridge Park is currently open for swimming. Temple Park and Westcliff Park are closed indefinitely as structures are repaired.

Cedar Ridge is a prime camping spot on Belton Lake. Partially forested and enhanced by white limestone bluffs, the park abounds with wildlife and springtime wildflowers. This is largely a no-frills park, best appreciated by families looking for no-fuss camping and pleasant swimming in a small, contained part of the lake.

SWIMMING: A small designated swim beach is located on the east side of the park. Look for a concrete walkway to the right of the parking lot that will lead you down a short, grassy decline to the pebbled beach. The sloping lawn ends in a strip of shoreline that offers walk-in access to the lake. Beneath the water, the pebbles give way to a relatively smooth, firm lake bed. The opaque water is about five to six feet into the swim area, depending on recent rainfall. The curving shoreline faces a scenic limestone bluff, and some shade is available. Day use is welcome.

AMENITIES: Restrooms with showers. Hiking trails. Basketball court. Playground. Marina. Seasonal restaurant and concession stand.

PRO TIP: Give the Temple Park office a call to keep up with its restoration and swim status: (254) 780-2461. Temple is a spacious park with many amenities and great access to the water. If it's open, definitely head there to celebrate its revival!

Cleburne State Park

5800 Park Road 21
Cleburne, TX 76033
(817) 645-4215
tpwd.texas.gov/state-parks/cleburne

HOURS: 7 a.m.–10 p.m.

ENTRANCE FEES: $5 per adult. Free ages 12 and under. Camping fees apply.

PARK RULES: Texas Parks & Wildlife rules apply. In addition, boats may create no wake. Personal watercraft (Jet Skis, Sea-Doos, etc.) prohibited.

CAMPING: Tent, RV (water and electric hookups), screened shelters, and group facilities. Waterfront camping available.

ABOUT: Located just over ten miles southwest of Cleburne (a small town south of Fort Worth), Cleburne State Park is a lush, 528-acre park surrounding spring-fed Cedar Lake. Developed by the CCC and opened to the public in 1938, this park offers much for visitors to enjoy, including camping, more than five miles of mountain bike trails, a picnic area built within a cove of ash and juniper trees, and convenient swim access to Cedar Lake, which was formed by an earthen dam constructed by the CCC. The drive to Cleburne State Park will take you down several backcountry roads. You'll feel a pleasant rural distance here.

SWIMMING: One of the great things about swimming at Cleburne is that this is a no-wake lake, which means motorized watercraft will not affect your swim experience. At the designated swim area, a wide grassy lawn gently slopes into a man-made sand beach. Walk right into the spring-fed lake and its sandy, firm bottom. The beach is unshaded, but plenty of tree shade isn't far away. Tall grass grows on the opposite bank. At the right time of year, this area is rich, green, and full of vibrant plant life. No lifeguard is on duty; swim at your own risk.

AMENITIES: Restrooms with showers. Picnic areas with grills. Playground. Sand volleyball courts. Group facilities.

PRO TIP: There's no park store at Cleburne. Outside amenities are a good distance away, so come prepared with supplies, particularly if you're planning to camp. While you're here, be sure to check out the three-tiered limestone spillway, a CCC point of pride.

Copper Breaks State Park

777 Park Road 62
Quanah, TX 79252
(940) 839-4331
tpwd.texas.gov/state-parks/copper-breaks

HOURS: 7 a.m.–10 p.m.
ENTRANCE FEES: $3 per adult. Free ages 12 and under. Camping fees apply.
PARK RULES: Texas Parks & Wildlife rules apply.
CAMPING: Primitive, tent, equestrian, and RV (water and electric hookups).

ABOUT: Established in 1970 on the plains a few hours north of Abilene, Copper Breaks State Park is a great place to feel far away from it all. This 1,900-acre park is notable for its abundant wildlife, natural terrain, and dark, star-filled nights far from the light pollution of any major town or city. (It has been designated an International Dark Sky Park.) Here you can hike the same grass-covered, copper-rich mesas once traversed by the Kiowa and Comanche tribes, not far from where Cynthia Ann Parker, mother of Quanah Parker, was recaptured from the Comanches to be returned to her original family. Bordered by the Pease River, the park offers fine views of red-rock canyons in the Caprock escarpment, whose walls give evidence of the shallow sea that once spread across much of Texas. (Look in the rock for the fossilized lips of sand pushed by waves.) Copper Breaks is a quiet, remote spot to experience a bit of wilderness and history.

While the park is open for day use, consider camping for the night to get the most out of your visit. The Comanche campground offers unique shelter structures on each site.

SWIMMING: A swim beach has been designated on Lake Copper Breaks, one of two lakes within the park. The bank is long, narrow, and grassy and slopes directly into the water. Wood posts mark off the swim area. The area behind the designated swim space is marshlike, with tall plants growing out of the water. The bottom is soft and spotted with vegetation. Swim shoes are recommended. No lifeguard is on duty; swim at your own risk. The other lake in the park, Big Pond, doesn't have a designated swim area.

AMENITIES: Restrooms with showers. Picnic tables with grills. Volleyball court. Group picnic area. Boat ramp. Multiuse trails for hiking, mountain biking, and horseback riding.

PRO TIP: Be sure to visit the interpretive center in the visitors' center, where you'll find an exhibit about the area's history, including information about Native American tribes, Quanah Parker, cowboy life, and ranching.

Dinosaur Valley State Park

1629 Park Road 59
Glen Rose, TX 76043
(254) 897-4588
tpwd.texas.gov/state-parks/dinosaur-valley

HOURS: 7 a.m.—10 p.m.

ENTRANCE FEES: $7 per adult. Free ages 12 and under. Camping fees apply.

PARK RULES: Texas Parks & Wildlife rules apply.

CAMPING: Primitive, tent, RV (water and electric hookups), screened shelters, and group facilities. A few waterfront spots available.

ABOUT: Swim with the dinosaurs! Well, not quite, but at Dinosaur Valley State Park, located approximately sixty miles southwest of Fort Worth, you can swim the Paluxy River, a branch of the Brazos. The eroded riverbed reveals tracks left by dinosaurs that roamed Central Texas more than a hundred million years ago, when the land was at the edge of a shallow ocean. Pick up a map at the visitors' booth and look for the tracks of theropods and brontosaurs and those of paluxysaurs, the official state dinosaur of Texas. Water levels will affect the number of tracks visible at a given time. You're likely to catch sight of the most tracks in late summer, though some may already be visible in mid-May, when the park also blooms with fields of bluebonnets.

You'll find many spots to dip into the crystal-clear water at 1,500-acre Dinosaur Valley, as well as twenty miles of hiking trails and opportunities for camping, horseback riding, and mountain biking. Be sure to stop for a photo with the statues of the tyrannosaurus rex and brontosaurus near the main entrance on your way in. They were part of Sinclair Oil's Dinoland exhibit at the 1964–1965 New York World's Fair.

SWIMMING: Take your pick of entry points into the blue, inviting Paluxy River. At Track Site #1, The Blue Hole, you'll find steep access to the water following trails that course a low, sandy cliff thick with trees and vegetation. The bank is narrow here and cannot easily accommodate a large crowd. The water is deep, fluctuating between twelve and twenty-one feet, so children and nonswimmers should have floats. Be prepared to climb in and out of the water. Also be prepared for a fantastic view of the river.

The prime swim spot is at Track Site #2, Main Track Site. Here the water runs shallow over an uneven rock bed. At this site you can walk across a line of slippery rocks to view a set of dinosaur tracks. A wheelchair ramp and stairs lead down from the parking area to a concrete pathway above a set of narrow limestone steps that take you down to the water's edge. No lifeguard is on duty at either spot; swim at your own risk.

AMENITIES: Restrooms with showers. Picnic areas with grills. Sand volleyball courts. Playground. Horseback riding in the equestrian area.

PRO TIP: Take a spin through the dinosaur exhibit in the visitors' center to read up on the massive creatures that once stomped across the vibrant landscape you're about to enter. And either before or after your park visit, check out Dinosaur World just down the road, an entertaining attraction with opportunities for kids to learn and play.

Fort Parker State Park

194 Park Road 28
Mexia, TX 76667
(254) 562-5751
tpwd.texas.gov/state-parks/fort-parker

HOURS: 8 a.m.—10 p.m.

ENTRANCE FEES: $4 per adult. Free ages 12 and under. Camping fees apply.

PARK RULES: Texas Parks & Wildlife rules apply.

CAMPING: Primitive, tent, RV (water and electric hookups), screened shelters, and group facilities.

ABOUT: Fort Parker State Park was built by an African American company of the CCC from 1935 to 1941. The former town of Springfield, which became a haven for freedmen during Reconstruction, was inundated by the creation of 750-acre Fort Parker Lake. The men of the CCC built a 423-foot dam of cement and limestone across the Navasota River, a mission that required hauling rock, digging out the footings and other dam features, and pouring the cement. When visiting, take a moment to appreciate the bathhouse, cement picnic tables, roads, and other features the CCC built using timber cleared during the construction of the dam. After their work on the park, many of the men were redirected to fight in World War II.

Old Fort Parker, whose stockade and cabins were replicated by the CCC for the Texas centennial in 1936, sits nearby and was the site of the 1836 Comanche raid during which young Cynthia Ann Parker, the mother of Quanah Parker, was first captured. Today, the park offers plentiful shade, an activity and nature center, several miles of hiking trails, and an unsupervised swim area. Springfield's cemetery still stands within the park and is open for self-guided tours.

SWIMMING: The wide, grassy banks of the swim area afford a tremendous view of Fort Parker Lake's 750 acres. A thin concrete lip marks the edge of the shoreline and must be stepped over to enter the shallow water. The lake bottom is soft. Plenty of shade is available near the shore, where you'll have no trouble finding a spot to spread a blanket and take in the phenomenal view of the lake.

AMENITIES: Restrooms with showers. Picnic areas with grills. Hike and bike trails. Canoe, kayak, and paddleboat rental. Discovery and nature center.

PRO TIP: The park offers many activities through its discovery center. Pick up a schedule at the visitors' center on your way in. For a unique hike, choose the two-mile Springfield Trail, which will take you through old Springfield Cemetery and by the natural springs that feed Lake Springfield.

Grapevine Lake

| lake-grapevine.com

ABOUT: Northeast of Fort Worth and northwest of Dallas, the ample shoreline at Grapevine Lake is popular with day-trippers and campers alike, offering opportunities for hiking, boating, paddling, swimming, and kicking back in its beautiful parks. Managed by the Army Corps of Engineers, Grapevine Lake is an impoundment of the Trinity River, and it serves both as a reservoir for nearby Grapevine and the Dallas–Fort Worth metroplex and as an 8,000-acre recreational lake for residents and visitors. The dam was completed in 1952 and, along with other lakes in the region, provides flood control for areas along the Trinity River. Management of the individual parks surrounding the lake varies; some are run by local communities and others fall within the purview of the Army Corps of Engineers. Grapevine Lake is a favorite spot in a region that also includes Lewisville Lake and Eagle Mountain Lake.

There are two designated swim areas at Grapevine Lake, though plenty of swimmers jump in along the shoreline in undesignated areas as well: Meadowmere Park (which suffered damage from flooding in 2016 and is closed at the time of printing); and Vineyard's Campgrounds, a privately owned campground that is open only to campers. Katie's Woods, located at the southern end of the park off Park Road 7 (near the Gaylord Convention Center), is a popular spot for swimming in a nondesignated area. No lifeguards are on duty in any of the parks; swim at your own risk. As this lake is part of a flood control system, be advised that heavy rain and flooding in the region will affect accessibility to the parks.

KATIE'S WOODS

1899 Katie's Woods Loop
Grapevine, Texas 76051
lake-grapevine.com/katies-woods-park

HOURS: 8 a.m. to dusk.
ENTRANCE FEES: Free. $5 fee for boat ramp.
PARK RULES: Glass containers and open fires (except for fire rings) prohibited. Pets must be on leash. Alcohol permitted.
CAMPING: Not available.
ABOUT: Plentiful trees offer a good amount of shade in this small park on the southeastern shore of Grapevine Lake. Hiking trails lead to cliffs with fantastic views of the lake. A limited number

of covered picnic tables are available, though they fill up quickly on busy weekends. American elms, live oaks, and cedar elms offer a bit of shade. If you're looking for a quiet, free place to grab a taste of Grapevine Lake, Katie's Woods can't be beat.

SWIMMING: While there is no designated swim beach at Katie's Woods, this small, wooded park remains popular for folks looking to take a quick dip in shallow water. A grassy, unshaded hill slopes down into a swim cove. The shoreline is quite rocky; swim shoes are recommended. The pebbles and stones give way to a sandy, mostly firm bottom. This is a popular lake for boats and Jet Skis, whose wakes are felt in shallow waves that lap the shore.

AMENITIES: Restrooms. Covered picnic tables with grills. Boat ramp.

MEADOWMERE PARK

3000 Meadowmere Lane
Grapevine, TX 76051
(817) 410-3470
lake-grapevine.com/meadowmere-park

HOURS: 8 a.m. to dusk.

ENTRANCE FEES: $5 per vehicle. $1 per pedestrian. Easter, Memorial Day, Independence Day, and Labor Day: $10 per vehicle. $2 per pedestrian. Camping fees apply.

PARK RULES: Glass containers and open fires (except for fire rings) prohibited. Pets must be on leash. Alcohol permitted.

CAMPING: Tent camping. Lakefront sites available.

ABOUT: Located on the lake's southwestern shore, this 252-acre park is typically the busiest on Grapevine Lake, thanks to its easy-access swimming and wooded hiking trails. Meadowmere Park was closed in 2016 due to flood damage, but it may be reopened by swim season 2017.

SWIMMING: A sandy shoreline faces a roped-off swim area. Plenty of green lawn stretches along the water, and several covered picnic tables sit close to the water. The curving bank slopes around the lake, offering easy walk-in access to the water. Step in and enjoy the view. Be aware that boat traffic will create a wake in the swim area.

AMENITIES: Clean and modern restrooms. Playscape. Low-water boat ramp. Kayak rentals. Volleyball courts. Horseshoe pits.

Lake Arrowhead State Park

229 Park Road 63
Wichita Falls, TX 76310
(940) 528-2211
tpwd.texas.gov/state-parks/lake-arrowhead

HOURS: 8 a.m.–10 p.m.
ENTRANCE FEES: $4 per adult. Free ages 12 and under. Camping fees apply.
PARK RULES: Texas Parks & Wildlife rules apply.
CAMPING: Tent, RV (water and electric hookups), and equestrian. Waterfront sites available.

ABOUT: Lake Arrowhead State Park is a 524-acre park located thirteen miles from Wichita Falls and approximately two hours west of Dallas. This spacious, wide open park has plenty of room to explore. Lake Arrowhead is located on the Little Wichita River, a tributary of the Red River, which earns its name from the iron-rich soil that tints the water red. Established as a reservoir, the lake offers plenty of recreational activities and a 106-mile-long lakeshore. Lake Arrowhead is one of the eastern-most points to see the black-tailed prairie dog, so abundant here that the park has designated a portion of its land as "Prairie Dog Town." Don't be surprised to run into other wildlife—geese make regular stops here and often make Lake Arrowhead their home.

SWIMMING: While the water is accessible from many spots along this long shoreline, the designated swim beach offers a roped-off swim area and long grassy bank. The water is typically crystal clear. No lifeguard is on duty; swim at your own risk.

AMENITIES: Covered picnic tables on concrete beds. Grills. Volleyball court. Group picnic area. Boat ramp. Hiking trails. Fishing. Water skiing. Horseback riding. Disc golf. Restrooms and showers.

PRO TIP: Make sure to visit Prairie Dog Town! Don't miss these little guys, who will bark greetings at you and generally delight as they go about their busy day.

Lake Brownwood State Park

200 State Highway Park Road 15
Lake Brownwood, TX 76801
(325) 784-5223
tpwd.texas.gov/state-parks/lake-brownwood

HOURS: 6 a.m.–10 p.m.

ENTRANCE FEES: $5 per adult. Free ages 12 and under. Camping fees apply.

PARK RULES: Texas Parks & Wildlife rules apply.

CAMPING: Tent, RV (water and electric hookups), and equestrian. Waterfront sites available.

ABOUT: Lake Brownwood State Park is a great place to feel far, far away from it all. Long country roads take you to this beautiful 537-acre park near the geographical center of Texas. Lake Brownwood was a CCC project, and the builders sourced local natural materials to construct the impressive recreation hall,

which includes an observation deck that offers a terrific view of the lake and surrounding area. The CCC also used rock from local quarries to build picnic tables, fire pits, cabins, outdoor patios, and more than one hundred other structures. Three miles of hiking trails are available here, including a walk that will take you to Council Bluff, where you get yet another fantastic view of the lake. The park offers plenty of camping space.

SWIMMING: The day-use swim area at Brownwood is set apart from the campsites. Here you'll find a long grassy bank, picnic tables set under the shade of live oak trees, and plenty of space to spread out. The grass extends right to the shoreline, where you can walk right into the lake. The lake bottom is sandy, with some vegetation. The water temperature is moderate in the summer. The swimming is easy at Lake Brownwood, as is the camping. No lifeguard is on duty; swim at your own risk.

AMENITIES: Restrooms with showers. Picnic tables. Boat ramps. Volleyball court. Hiking trails.

PRO TIP: Find a great view of the lake from the Council Bluff Pavilion and Overlook.

Lewisville Lake

lake-lewisville.org

ABOUT: Nestled between Flower Mound and Denton, Lewisville Lake is one of the largest lakes in North Texas. With 233 miles of shoreline and 29,000 acres of water, this reservoir is a popular site for a variety of water activities. The lake, which is operated by the Army Corps of Engineers, is formed by Lewisville Dam, which manages the flow of the Elm Fork of the Trinity River upstream of Fort Worth and Dallas. Completed in 1955, the dam was part of a series of projects that combined existing reservoirs and sought to improve flood prevention and water storage. The lake underwent a few name changes over the years. Beginning its life as Lake Dallas, it was eventually renamed Lewisville Lake in the mid-1970s.

A few specific parks around the lake offer the best swimming: Little Elm Park, Pilot Knoll Park, and Stewart Creek Park. Some of these spots truck in sand to augment the shoreline, creating unique, beachlike swim experiences. Heavy rain does flood Lewisville Lake on occasion. Lake Park, a popular spot on Lewisville over the years, suffered severe damage from flooding in 2016 and has been closed indefinitely.

LITTLE ELM PARK

701 West Eldorado Parkway
Little Elm, TX 75068
lake-lewisville.org/little-elm-park

HOURS: Open 24/7.
ENTRANCE FEES: Sa–Su $10 parking fee (Memorial Day through Labor Day); seasonal passes available; fees for boat ramp and camping apply.

PARK RULES: Swim in designated areas only. Glass and grills prohibited on beach. Pets must be on leash and are not permitted on beach. No camping on beach. No fishing from beach.

CAMPING: Tent camping.

ABOUT: With a sandy shoreline, snack bar, sand volleyball court, a boat ramp, and a huge swim area, Little Elm Park has a distinct beach feel. A great place for kids and anyone looking for easy access to the water, this highly popular spot can fill up quickly in the warm months with good reason—swimming here is easy and comfortable, and the amenities abound.

SWIMMING: The extensive swim area is roped off, so there's no need to worry about boat, kayak, or paddleboard traffic interfering with your swim. For added safety, you can borrow one of the life jackets on loan at no charge at a kiosk near the shore. The water is wheelchair accessible.

AMENITIES: Restrooms. Barbecue grills. Snack grill (hours vary). Pavilion with covered picnic tables. Playground. Sand volleyball courts (no reservations required).

PRO TIP: On the weekends the town of Little Elm offers EFrogs, an electric shuttle service that gives complimentary rides around the lakefront district. Visit lakefrontlittleelm.com /gallery/efrog for information. Remember to tip your driver!

PILOT KNOLL PARK

218A Orchid Hill Road
Argyle, TX 76226
lake-lewisville.org/pilot-knoll-park

HOURS: 10 a.m.–4 p.m.

ENTRANCE FEES: $10 per vehicle.

PARK RULES: Motorized vehicles, alcohol, fireworks, littering, firearms, fires outside of barbecue grills prohibited. Pets must be on leash.

CAMPING: Primitive, tent, and RV. Campers set up at the northern end of the park.

ABOUT: The day-use area of the park with access to Lewisville Lake covers roughly 70 acres at the southern tip of the park, on the west side of the lake. Covered picnic tables are well spaced, often close to individual parking spots, so that visitors can enjoy a bit of individual space.

SWIMMING: Several grassy arms extend into the lake off the curving shoreline, creating a series of small nooks and coves for swimming. The roped-off swim area is large. Walk right into the water, where a soft bottom will meet your feet. Visitors enjoy an expansive view of the lake from the shores of Pilot Knoll Park. While there's plenty of space to spread out, keep in mind that the lawn is largely unshaded.

AMENITIES: Restrooms. Picnic tables with grills. Volleyball court. Horseshoe pit. Equestrian trails. Kayak and boat rentals. Boat ramp. Pavilions.

PRO TIP: Hop over to Denton, just about ten miles north of Pilot Knoll Park, and hang out in this college town's casual-hip coffee shops, bookstores, restaurants, and bars.

STEWART CREEK PARK

3700 Sparks Road
The Colony, TX 75056
lake-lewisville.org/stewart-creek-park

HOURS: 6 a.m.–10 p.m.

ENTRANCE FEES: $10 per vehicle. Camping fees apply.

PARK RULES: Obey all posted rules.

CAMPING: Tent and RV only with the purchase of an annual permit.

ABOUT: Stewart Creek Park is a great place for day swimming on the eastern shore of Lewisville Lake. Owned by the City of the

Colony, a growing community of residential and retail developments, the park is accessed through a residential neighborhood. Stop at the booth, pay the entry fee, and then head down a paved road. Parking rings a grassy area, so you can drive in and park close to your preferred spot.

SWIMMING: Typically boasting thirty to fifty feet of sandy shoreline, the wide grassy space slopes directly into the lake, with a pleasant view of surrounding lakeshore. Plenty of picnic tables and open spaces offer room to post up and relax for the day. There is some shade in the park close to the water, but this area is mostly exposed, so be sure to bring your sunscreen.

AMENITIES: Picnic tables with grills. Boat ramps. Horseshoe pits. Sand volleyball court. Hiking trails.

Lake Mineral Wells State Park

100 Park Road 71
Mineral Wells, TX 76067
(940) 328-1171
tpwd.texas.gov/state-parks/lake-mineral-wells

HOURS: 6 a.m.–10 p.m.

ENTRANCE FEES: $7 per adult. Free ages 12 and under. Camping fees apply.

PARK RULES: Texas Parks & Wildlife rules apply.

CAMPING: Primitive, tent, and RV (water and electric hookups). Waterfront sites available.

ABOUT: In the late 1880s settler James Alvin Lynch drew water from a well at what is now Mineral Wells that he claimed cured his wife's rheumatism. Word spread of the water's healing properties, and soon the town was a booming health resort and tourist destination. The area's population skyrocketed, thus draining the very water resources people came to enjoy. Fast-forward more than one hundred years, and the town of Mineral Wells is now a typical suburb that still boasts a body of water that draws visitors year after year to refresh and rejuvenate. Lake Mineral Wells is an impounded portion of Rock Creek, a tributary of the Brazos River. Forty-five minutes west of Fort Worth, the 640-acre park surrounding the lake is popular for swimming, hiking, and rock climbing and is just a short drive from city life.

The park is also the terminus of Lake Mineral Wells Trailway, a twenty-mile-long reclaimed railroad bed. Running from northwest of Weatherford to downtown Mineral Wells, the Trailway can be accessed from four trailheads and features fifteen bridges, including a five-hundred-foot-long bridge that carries hikers over Highway 180. The rail bed is a remnant of the days when Mineral Wells was a hopping tourist destination.

SWIMMING: A wide, man-made sand beach lines the lakeshore at the designated swim area. The buoyed-off swim area is quite large, with a firm sand bottom. The water isn't too cold in summer, and the lake bottom has a steady grade from shallow to deeper waters. Walk right into the lake from the shore and enjoy an easy swim. No lifeguard is on duty; swim at your own risk.

AMENITIES: Restrooms with showers. Picnic tables with grills. Group picnic area. Boat ramp. Hiking trails. Fishing. Water skiing. Scuba diving. Snorkeling. Park store with groceries, supplies, and souvenirs. Note: Visitors must bring their own water for consumption; the water here is nonpotable due to high salt content.

PRO TIP: Visit the nearby well where they've been bottling mineral water for over one hundred years. The Famous Mineral Water Co. is now known as Crazy Water. They'll give you a tour and let you fill your own jug directly from the well.

Possum Kingdom State Park

3901 Park Road 33
PO Box 70
Caddo, TX 76429
(940) 549-1803
tpwd.texas.gov/state-parks/possum-kingdom

HOURS: 8 a.m.–10 p.m.
ENTRANCE FEES: $4 per adult. Free ages 12 and under. Camping fees apply.
PARK RULES: Texas Parks & Wildlife rules apply.
CAMPING: Primitive, tent, RV (water and electric hookups), and air-conditioned cabins.

ABOUT: Head an hour west of the Dallas–Fort Worth metroplex and you'll discover one of the area's most celebrated state parks, located in the canyons of the Palo Pinto Mountains. The clear blue waters of Possum Kingdom Lake are a popular place to kick back and enjoy lake life against a scenic backdrop. With more than 1,500 acres of land, 20,000 acres of water, three hundred miles of shoreline, and amenities built by the CCC, this park has kept visitors coming back year after year since it opened to the public in 1950. You'll find plenty of coves to explore and impressive limestone cliffs at the park's southeast end. Near the day-use area a convenient park store provides groceries, supplies, and souvenirs.

SWIMMING: Possum Kingdom Lake is a terrific place to swim. A large designated swim area is roped off with buoys against a long, wide grassy bank. Depending on lake levels, you may have to step off the bank and into the water—the shore doesn't necessarily slope directly into the lake. The bottom is firm, sandy, and rocky. There's plenty of space to spread out here and plenty of room to swim in view of the surrounding hills. Shade is limited, though covered picnic tables are available on the grass. This is an easy, refreshing place to get in the water. No lifeguard is on duty; swim at your own risk.

AMENITIES: Restrooms with showers. Picnic tables with grills. Group picnic area. Boat ramp. Canoe and kayak rentals. Hiking trails. Fishing. Water skiing. Scuba diving. Snorkeling. Park store. Note: Visitors must bring their own water for consumption; the water here is nonpotable due to high salt content.

PRO TIP: If the state park is full, check out one of the ten Brazos River Authority parks on Possum Kingdom Lake for more camping and water access.

NORTH

Ray Roberts Lake State Park

| **tpwd.texas.gov/state-parks/ray-roberts-lake**

HOURS: 6 a.m.–10 p.m.

ENTRANCE FEES: $7 per adult. Free ages 12 and under. Camping fees apply.

PARK RULES: Texas Parks & Wildlife rules apply.

CAMPING: Tent, RV (water and electric hookups), screened shelters, and group sites.

ABOUT: Just north of Denton and only an hour north of the Dallas–Fort Worth metroplex is a unique park in small Pilot Point, on an impounded part of the Trinity River. Covering 29,000 acres and three different ecoregions, Ray Roberts Lake State Park encompasses multiple units surrounding the lake. The park incorporates sections of the Blackland Prairie, the Grand Prairie, and the Eastern Cross Timbers ecoregions. The resulting natural environment features abundant and diverse flora and fauna that offer different experiences depending on which area of the lake you visit. Archaeological evidence indicates that the area was used by hunters and gatherers more than eleven thousand years ago. Radiocarbon dating of artifacts found at the nearby Aubrey Clovis archaeological site indicates that Paleo-Americans lived in the area for millennia.

Ray Roberts Lake is one of twenty-two reservoirs impounded on the Trinity River. In addition to offering multiple recreational activities, it also provides water for Dallas and Denton. This is a terrific park for camping close to Denton.

While all but one of the park's units (the twenty-mile Greenbelt Corridor, which runs all the way down to Lewisville Lake) have lake access, only two have designated swim areas: the Isle du Bois Unit on the south side of the lake and the Johnson Branch Unit on the north side.

ISLE DU BOIS UNIT

100 PW 4137
Pilot Point, TX 76258
(940) 686-2148

SWIMMING: Isle du Bois is the larger, more popular swim area on Ray Roberts Lake. An extensive sand beach curves around the water, backed by a large green lawn with paved concrete walkways connecting covered picnic areas with grills. The water is clear and inviting. Walk right in on a sandy, firm bottom and take in the wide view of the park's opposing shores. The roped-off swim area is quite spacious, as is the natural area where you can spread out and set up for the day. A grassy hill to the right

offers plenty of shade, along with additional covered picnic tables. No lifeguard is on duty; swim at your own risk.

AMENITIES: Restrooms with showers. Picnic areas with grills. Volleyball court. Boat ramp.

PRO TIP: Take a spin through Pilot Point's small square, where you'll find a whiskey and gin distillery open regularly for tastings and some great outdoor murals perfect for photo ops. Be sure to stop in at Lowbrow's Beer and Wine Garden, a tavern in the center of Pilot Point housed inside the former site of the town's newspaper offices.

JOHNSON BRANCH UNIT

100 PW 4153
Valley View, TX 76272
(940) 637-2294

SWIMMING: With a grassy shoreline curving down to a roped-off swim area, the Johnson Branch Unit offers a nearly identical swim experience to the Isle du Bois Unit, though the beach is slightly smaller. Because it's located on the north side of the lake and is a farther drive from the Dallas–Fort Worth metroplex, the Johnson Branch Unit can be a bit quieter than Isle du Bois. No lifeguard is on duty; swim at your own risk.

AMENITIES: Restrooms with showers. Picnic areas with grills. Volleyball court. Boat ramp.

Stillhouse Park

4050 Simmons Road
Belton, TX 76513
(254) 939-2461
swf-wc.usace.army.mil/stillhouse/index.asp

HOURS: 10 a.m.–8 p.m. (Mar.–Sep.).

ENTRANCE FEES: $5 per vehicle.

PARK RULES: Fireworks and off-road vehicles prohibited. Pets must be on leash.

CAMPING: Not available.

ABOUT: Located just about an hour north of Austin and just south of Waco, Stillhouse Hollow Lake is an impoundment of

the Lampasas River created in the early 1960s for purposes of flood control. The Army Corps of Engineers owns and manages the recreational facilities around the lake, which include some terrific spots to swim. Although flooding in 2016 has affected the status of some of the parks surrounding Stillhouse Lake, Stillhouse Park remains open for swimming and recreation. Drive down the paved road from the entrance booth and keep your cameras up as an impressive view of the water opens up below. There's a spot to pull off and grab a scenic photo before heading down to the day-use area, where you'll find ample green grass to spread out. This is a big, beautiful, well-maintained park with a long, curving shoreline and a distinctly beachlike feel. Shade is limited.

SWIMMING: Walk-in access to the blue-green water is plentiful. Pebbles line the shore and cover the lake bottom; water shoes are recommended. The water deepens fairly quickly. Depending on where you get in, you'll either have a view of the Stillhouse Hollow Dam or of the surrounding undeveloped banks and the small wooded island not far from shore. You will notice wake from recreational boats and Jet Skis on the lake.

AMENITIES: Restrooms. Picnic tables. Grills. Volleyball court. Group picnic area. Boat ramp.

PRO TIP: Explore the other parks around Stillhouse Hollow Lake. Chalk Ridge Falls Park offers more than five miles of trails, including hikes that take you past some impressive waterfalls.

Twin Points Park at Eagle Mountain Lake

10000 Ten Mile Bridge Road
Fort Worth, TX 76135
eaglemountainlake.org/twin-points-park

HOURS: 10 a.m.–7 p.m. (Memorial Day through Labor Day).

ENTRANCE FEES: $20 per vehicle. $40 for passenger vans. $5 for motorcycles and bicycles. Half price M–Th, except for holidays and special events.

PARK RULES: Pets, glass, littering, smoking, alcohol, bicycles, skateboards, hoverboards, commercial photography, attaching hammocks to trees or structures, open fires, vulgar or offensive acts or language prohibited. Ages 12 and under must be accompanied by an adult.

CAMPING: Not available.

ABOUT: Located on Fort Worth's 8,694-acre Eagle Mountain Lake, Twin Points Park is a modern, manicured recreational facility with a large, beachlike swim area that's well worth the price of admission, particularly if you're bringing a full carload. The park was a privately owned resort until 2007, when its lease wasn't renewed. At that point a multiphase plan to renovate and update the park and its beloved swimming area was put into effect by the Tarrant Regional Water District. The plan was fulfilled in 2016 when the park opened in time for Memorial Day weekend.

A large parking lot sits at the top of a gentle hill that eases down a long, wide, grassy lawn to the sandy shoreline. The park is meticulously landscaped: a concrete walkway winds down the lawn, and trees offer a limited amount of shade. Just northwest of downtown Fort Worth, this is a highly popular destination that local Texans are thrilled to see operating once again. It's quite busy on the weekends, so be prepared for a crowd if you visit during peak hours.

SWIMMING: The sandy shoreline and walk-in access to the water create a distinctly beachlike experience. The roped-off swim area is quite large and includes a stationary dock within swimming distance of the shore. To the right of the natural shoreline, a half-moon concrete lip gives swimmers a place to sit and dangle their feet in the water. The lake bottom is firm and sandy, and the water temperature is moderate. This is a great swim spot for kids, and there's plenty of room in the water for everyone.

AMENITIES: Modern and well-maintained restrooms. Covered picnic areas. Boat ramp. Volleyball courts.

PRO TIP: For a quiet, low-key swim experience on Eagle Mountain Lake, check out Shady Grove Park. This 24-acre park on the southwest shore of the lake provides several amenities, including a stretch of beach at the back of the park with a roped-off swim area. There isn't much else happening way out on this stretch of Highway 199 West, so it's lighter on the tourists.

East

Welcome to East Texas, the part of the Lone Star State behind the pine curtain. Out here you'll find redolent Pineywoods and Big Thicket forests stretching tall trunks toward big blue skies. More than thirty lakes live in the eastern portion of the state, many of them offering shady campsites with soft pine breezes (and some of them home to alligators—give the park signs a thorough read). This is also the part of Texas where you'll find, per capita,* the most donut shops in the state. (*Calculations unofficial, but likely.) Small towns abound, as do shaded spots to swim, picnic, and wonder if you didn't somehow transport yourself to the Pacific Northwest by following an unexpected back road. Not to be missed out here: Daingerfield State Park, an idyllic lake swim with nothing for the eye to see but rich forest in the summer and changing leaves in the fall.

Important to note about East Texas: in addition to its stunning forests, it's home to several power plants, many of which use impounded lake water for cooling. These lakes are also used for recreational purposes such as fishing and swimming. This practice is not unique to Texas, and its primary effect is warming the water. This guide includes at least one such park in Texas, Coleto Creek, which falls in the South Texas region.

LONGVIEW

TYLER

CORSICANA

NACODOCHES

COLLEGE
STATION

THE SWIMMING
HOLES OF
East Texas

1 Boykin Springs Recreation
  Area, Angelina National
  Forest
2 Daingerfield State Park
3 Fort Boggy State Park
4 Huntsville State Park
5 Lake Bob Sandlin State Park

6 Lake Livingston State Park
7 Lake Tejas
8 Martin Dies Jr. State Park
9 Ratcliff Recreation Area,
  Davy Crockett National
  Forest
10 Tyler State Park

Boykin Springs Recreation Area, Angelina National Forest

Forest Road 313
Zavalla, TX 75980
(936) 897-1068
recreation.gov

HOURS: 6 a.m.–10 p.m.

ENTRANCE FEES: Free. Camping fees apply.

PARK RULES: National park rules apply. Obey all posted signs.

CAMPING: Tent, RV, cabins, and group sites. Waterfront sites available.

ABOUT: Angelina National Forest is one of four national forests in Texas established by President Franklin D. Roosevelt in the 1930s. More than 150,000 acres surround the massive Sam Rayburn Reservoir, covering portions of four different counties with longleaf, loblolly, and shortleaf pines. Several recreation areas with campgrounds have been developed within the national forest. About ten miles east of Zavalla, Boykin Springs Recreation Area holds a 9-acre spring-fed lake that's the centerpiece of CCC work; you'll also find a sweet little swim spot at the mouth of a creek bed; follow the creek and it will deliver you to two secret swim holes. This sprawling park affords plenty to explore. Lace up your hiking boots while your swimsuit dries and get lost in the towering piney woods.

SWIMMING: To get to Boykin Springs Lake, hang a right just past the fee station on Forest Route 313. This small, quiet lake has a rocky bottom and is surrounded by forest, offering a serene, all-natural swim experience.

On the other side of the road, near a CCC-built picnic pavilion, is Boykin Creek, which will lead you to three neat little swimming holes in close proximity. Head to the right of the

parking lot and keep an eye out for the path down the bank to the shallow creek bed. Down here, on your left, you'll see a small spring-fed swimming hole that's completely undeveloped and unsupervised, nestled at the nexus of narrow natural conduits for the water. This spot is popular with campers. The water is shallow, though opaque, so visitors should take care while walking in the swim hole—the bottom consists of large, uneven boulders that drop off without warning.

AMENITIES: Restrooms with showers. Picnic areas. Picnic pavilion.

PRO TIP: Head past the small sand hill that rises up to the right of the swim hole and take a short walk down Boykin Creek. Watch for the source of Boykin Springs, located above the clay-and-boulder bank rising up on the right. Continue past the springs and you'll come to a fork, each arm of which leads to a gorgeous, cozy chest-deep swimming hole.

Daingerfield State Park

455 Park Road 17
Daingerfield, TX 75638
(903) 645-2921
tpwd.texas.gov/state-parks/daingerfield

HOURS: 8 a.m.–9 p.m.
ENTRANCE FEES: $4 per adult. Free ages 12 and under.
PARK RULES: Texas Parks & Wildlife rules apply.
CAMPING: Tent, RV (water and electric hookups), cabins, and group facilities. Waterfront sites available.
ABOUT: Southwest of Texarkana in the East Texas Pineywoods is one of the rare places in the state where visitors can appreciate a change in seasons and, when swim season is over, catch a bit of vibrant, colorful fall foliage. Daingerfield State Park's 500 acres are home to a natural environment abundant with plants and wildlife, including a wide variety of bird species. In the 1930s the CCC excavated land in the Cypress Creek drainage basin and built an earthen dam to impound the spring there, then created the park around the resulting lake.

Every design element at Daingerfield is intentional. The paved road that winds from the park entrance to the visitors' center was made to meander so that visitors have an opportunity to make the transition from the main road and busy modern life into the solitude and beauty of the forest. The park's activity areas are concentrated in an effort to preserve as much of the native landscape as possible in its undeveloped state. This attention to the natural world and experiential detail is true down to the star-shaped portholes cut in the patio walls at the Combination Building, as well as its open frames, which create both small and broad views of the lake.

SWIMMING: Swimming at Daingerfield is a transporting experience. The glassy lake is surrounded by forest, with no man-made

structure in sight but the CCC-built bathhouse. Straight across from the swim area is what looks like an island of forest—a cluster of trees nestled on a small peninsula. The lake is small, giving this swim spot a cozy, tucked-in feeling. Fish do live in this water, and some small- to moderate-sized fish will swim near the sets of stone steps that lead into the water. A swim platform floats a few dozen yards from the shoreline, where the water is over six feet deep on average. The lake bottom is soft and sandy, and the water is a moderate temperature in the summer. This is the dream lake experience.

AMENITIES: Restrooms with showers. Picnic area with grills. Hiking trails. Gift shop. Interpretive center.

PRO TIP: The tip is to just get yourself here. Daingerfield is one of the best swim spots in Texas.

Fort Boggy State Park

4994 Highway 75 South
Centerville, TX 75833
(903) 344-1116
tpwd.texas.gov/state-parks/fort-boggy

HOURS: 8 a.m.–10 p.m.

ENTRANCE FEES: $3 per adult. Free ages 12 and under.

PARK RULES: Texas Parks & Wildlife rules apply.

CAMPING: Not available.

ABOUT: This sweet spot on the edge of East Texas two hours northwest of Houston is a shaded haven for swimmers and picnickers. Located between the small towns of Leona and Centerville, Fort Boggy is a pretty 1,847-acre park and nature preserve with a small 15-acre lake where live oak, pecan, and post oak trees grow nearly to the edge of the water and offer a

shaded day-use area. Picnic tables sit on concrete slabs lined with low stone perimeters. Enjoy a hike on the park's trails, but be sure to keep to those designated trails, as this is a nature preserve and conservation is paramount. The park is named for a log blockhouse known as Fort Boggy that was built by Texas Rangers in 1839, purported to be the area's first settlers' building. The blockhouse is gone, but the name remains.

SWIMMING: The water here is relatively warm in summer and offers easy walk-in access from the sloping shore. The sandy lake bottom is firm with some vegetation. This spot is remarkable for its cozy, picturesque surroundings, and you can swim with a view of nothing but trees. Fort Boggy is a little pocket of peace and quiet. No lifeguard is on duty; swim at your own risk.

AMENITIES: Restrooms. Picnic tables. Picnic pavilion. Boat ramp. Fishing dock. Hiking trials.

PRO TIP: The park earns the nickname "Fort Buggy" as the warm seasons come on. Bring bug spray!

Huntsville State Park

565 Park Road 40 West
Huntsville, TX 77340
(936) 295-5644
tpwd.texas.gov/state-parks/huntsville

HOURS: 7 a.m.–10 p.m.

ENTRANCE FEES: $7 per adult. Free ages 12 and under.

PARK RULES: Texas Parks & Wildlife rules apply.

CAMPING: Tent, RV (water and electric hookups), and screened shelters. Waterfront sites available.

ABOUT: Its proximity to Houston makes Huntsville an extremely

popular park. On summer weekends the swim and picnic areas are packed with people splashing in the water, grilling lunch, lounging in hammocks, and enjoying time with family and friends. The floating dock is a popular jungle gym and launching pad for young swimmers. Students from nearby Sam Houston State University also frequent this spot to take a break from studying. Expect to hear music playing from pop-up tents in the busy picnic area, where visitors also take advantage of the shade from tall pines.

The park is the work of a CCC unit composed of African American veterans who reforested the heavily logged area with a variety of trees, built the original dam that created the lake, and constructed a recreation hall and other features.

SWIMMING: A sandy beach stretches into the water, where your feet will meet firm sand. While there's plenty of shade elsewhere in the day-use area, there is no shade on the beach. The swim area is buoyed off and includes a popular floating dock. On a busy summer weekend, the water is bright with floaties. No lifeguard is on duty; swim at your own risk.

Be aware that alligators do live in this park. Read all of the alligator safety and etiquette tips at the visitors' center when you arrive.

AMENITIES: Restrooms with showers. Picnic area. Boat ramp.

PRO TIP: Be prepared to share space and be friendly. Who knows? You may meet a new pal here.

Lake Bob Sandlin State Park

341 State Park Road 2117
Pittsburg, TX 75686
(903) 572-5531
tpwd.texas.gov/state-parks/lake-bob-sandlin

HOURS: 8 a.m.–9 p.m.

ENTRANCE FEES: $4 per adult. Free ages 12 and under. Camping fees apply.

PARK RULES: Texas Parks & Wildlife rules apply.

CAMPING: Tent, RV (water and electric hookups), and screened shelters. Waterfront sites available.

ABOUT: Entering Lake Bob Sandlin State Park feels a bit like entering another dimension, one in which the tall East Texas Pineywoods offer privacy, shade, seclusion, and beauty, and one where little obstructs a comfortable experience with the natural world. Be warned that you may be reluctant to rejoin life beyond the park gates once you're out here. Midway between Dallas and Texarkana and just south of I-30, Lake Bob Sandlin was formed in the mid-1970s when Fort Sherman Dam was built on Big Cypress Creek to create a reservoir for the surrounding counties. The 9,400-acre lake reaches a depth of sixty-five feet. It's not unusual to come across artifacts from the Native American tribes who lived here over the centuries. Hike the Lakeview Loop to see the ruins of Fort Sherman, built by the army of the Republic of Texas, as well as the Fort Sherman Cemetery, one of the oldest in the area. Bob Sandlin Park is as rich with history as it is with natural beauty.

SWIMMING: Swimming at Lake Bob Sandlin is as idyllic as its camping. From the grassy shore, enjoy a tremendous view of the lake. The beach is at the bottom of a shady hill that ends in an exposed grassy area marked off by a low stone wall. A narrow concrete path runs between the grass and the water, and a wooden ledge lets you sit and slip into the lake. Access is also available via wooden stairs that descend from the fishing dock to the right of the swim area. Use caution as you get in—those steps can be slick with algae. There isn't a shallow wading area; the water gets deep a few feet from shore. The bottom of the lake is pebbled and sandy and mostly firm. The water temperature is moderate in the summer months. A swim platform floats not too far from shore. No lifeguard is on duty; swim at your own risk. AMENITIES: Restrooms with showers. Picnic area with grills. Hiking and mountain biking trails.

PRO TIP: Camping here can feel quite private, thanks to a buffer of forest between sites. If possible, snag one of the many spots that sit on the edge of the lake and enjoy the serene sound of lapping water and the cooling lake breeze while you relax beneath the shade of the tall hardwoods and pines.

Lake Livingston State Park

300 Park Road 65
Livingston, TX 77351
(936) 365-2201
tpwd.texas.gov/state-parks/lake-livingston

HOURS: 8 a.m.–10 p.m.

ENTRANCE FEES: $5 per adult. Free ages 12 and under.

PARK RULES: Texas Parks & Wildlife rules apply.

CAMPING: Tent, RV (water and electric hookups), screened shelters, and group facilities. Waterfront sites available.

ABOUT: Located an hour north of Houston in the East Texas

Pineywoods, Lake Livingston State Park is a large park popular for swimming, paddling, and camping. Day use here is heavy on summer weekends, when folks congregate to dive in the water, grill up lunch, and run around in the ample grassy space. The lake itself, one of the largest reservoirs in Texas, is an impoundment of the Trinity River. This is a great place to bring the family to camp, with plenty of parkwide activities and natural areas to explore. The grassy peninsula in the day-use area provides good space for large groups to post up.

A recreation hall at the top of the day-use area was built with wide wooden steps and a significant stretch of awning that provides some shade. Shade elsewhere in this area is limited. Be aware that alligators do live in this park. Read all of the alligator safety and etiquette tips at the visitors' center when you arrive.

SWIMMING: One of the most important things to note about Lake Livingston is that the water is deep. Descending the metal ladders off the main bulkhead in the peninsula's cove immediately puts you in about five to six feet of water. Life jackets and floats for young swimmers are a must in this zone, and they aren't a bad idea for grown-up swimmers either. A concrete path runs the length of the long, curving peninsula shoreline and offers multiple points of access to the water via those ladders.

The best spot for kids is a gravel shore in the same area that gradually slopes into shallow water. If you have small swimmers with you, ask a park ranger to point you to this safer area to swim. No lifeguard on duty; swim at your own risk.

AMENITIES: Restrooms with showers. Picnic area. Boat ramp. Fishing pier. Amphitheater for rent. Pavilion. Park store. Playground. Canoe, kayak, and paddleboard rentals.

PRO TIP: Bring your own shade to make the most of the peninsula's extensive grassy area.

Lake Tejas

FM 256 East
Colmesneil, TX 75938
(409) 837-2063
laketejas.net

HOURS: M–Th 10 a.m.–6 p.m., F–Sa 10 a.m.–7 p.m., Su 12 p.m.–6 p.m. (Memorial Day through Labor Day).

ENTRANCE FEES: $6 per person. Free ages 3 and under. Cash and credit cards accepted. Additional fees for camping, picnic tables, and shelters.

PARK RULES: Alcohol, diapers in the lake, pets, glass, and smoking prohibited in the swimming area. No coolers or outside food or drink allowed inside the fenced swimming area. Additional rules apply, including regulations regarding the diving tower, slides, and boats. Visit the website for a full list of rules and regulations.

CAMPING: Tent, RV (water and electric hookups), and cabins. Campgrounds are open year round.

ABOUT: Are you ready to have some fun? Saddle up the kids and

head on out to Lake Tejas in East Texas. About 115 miles north-east of Houston, this is a spot where the whole family can spend the day enjoying two simple water slides, a wooden diving tower, two floating docks, a concession stand, and nonstop tunes from a countrified outdoor jukebox. Lake Tejas has long been a welcom-ing, family-friendly spot to hang out for a day or to stay overnight. The lake is currently owned by the Colmesneil School District.

SWIMMING: A long, white sand beach stretches along the shore. Walk right into the roped-off swim area and enjoy a shallow wading zone with young swimmers or head in a bit deeper. The bottom is firm and sandy and the water is warm in the summer. Enjoy the adventure of the tall slide and diving tower on the right, each with its own roped-off landing zone to keep adven-turers from colliding. A swim platform sits ready for cannon-balls. For smaller swimmers there's also a short slide with its own shallow, roped-off square of water. Lifeguards are on duty.

AMENITIES: Restrooms with showers. Swimming area picnic tables available to rent. Locker rentals. Boat, inner tube, and life jacket rentals. Concessions. Don't miss that jukebox!

PRO TIP: Talk to the crew here; the staff is quite pleasant and wants you to have a good time! Ask them how the park earned its name.

Martin Dies Jr. State Park

634 Park Road 48 South
Jasper, TX 75951
(409) 384-5231
tpwd.texas.gov/state-parks/martin-dies-jr

HOURS: 8 a.m.–10 p.m.
ENTRANCE FEES: $4 per adult. Free ages 12 and under.
PARK RULES: Texas Parks & Wildlife rules apply.
CAMPING: Tent, RV (water and electric hookups), screened shelters, and cabins. A group hall with kitchen. Waterfront sites available.

ABOUT: Martin Dies Jr. State Park spans the counties of Jasper and Woodsville at the northern edge of the Big Thicket National Preserve in the East Texas Pineywoods, where the Neches and Angelina Rivers join. Its 730 acres offer three different units that provide recreational access to eight miles of hiking trails, the 10,600-acre B. A. Steinhagen Reservoir, and several sloughs that run through the park. The park's unique layout and its abundant waterways create a unique ecological environment in which a wide variety of trees, including bald cypresses, pines, magnolias, and other varieties unique to this area of Texas offer shade and shelter for a diverse body of wildlife.

Martin Dies is well known for its paddling trails and guided canoe and kayak tours that take paddlers through preserved, untouched areas on waters occupied by alligators. Yes, alligators. Be sure to mind the alligator etiquette safety tips posted in the park, which include an important warning not to feed or harass the alligators. Check in with park rangers if you have any questions about alligator safety or behavior.

SWIMMING: The swim area at Martin Dies is located on the western side of the Hen House Ridge Unit. A variety of trees, including oaks hung with Spanish moss, grow on a large grassy lawn that rolls gently down toward the water. There's plenty of fine, flat space to spread out, though not all of it is shaded. Stone ramps with wood railings lead down the bank and into the roped-off swim area, offering easy access to water that rises to about two to three feet by the end of the ramp. The sandy bottom is firm, and the water is warm. This is a shallow lake. While clean, the water is typically murky. No lifeguard is on duty; swim at your own risk.

AMENITIES: Restrooms with showers. Picnic area with grills. Hiking and mountain biking trails. Canoe and kayak rentals. Guided paddling tours.

PRO TIP: Martin Dies is known as one of the best paddling destinations in Texas. Take a guided paddling tour and discover all this unique park has to offer.

Ratcliff Recreation Area, Davy Crockett National Forest

18551 State Highway 7 East
Kennard, TX 75487
(936) 655-2299
recreation.gov

HOURS: 6 a.m.–10 p.m.

ENTRANCE FEES: $5 per vehicle. Cash only. Pay at the self-pay station on the way into the park.

PARK RULES: National park rules apply. Alcohol allowed only at picnic tables in the day-use area. No pets in the swim area.

CAMPING: Tent, RV (water and electric hookups), and cabins. Sites are first come, first served. Waterfront sites available.

ABOUT: Driving through Davy Crockett National Forest toward Ratcliff Lake, you may feel as though you've left Texas altogether and entered the Pacific Northwest. Tall, skinny loblolly pines reach up to the clouds and drop pine needles and pinecones that blanket the ground underfoot. This peaceful forest, which also features oaks and other hardwood trees as well as abundant wildlife, is a peaceful, distant respite from the rest of the world. Ratcliff Recreation Area was a project of the CCC, which took on the area after the original lake had been used as a source of water for logging for several years. The CCC built an earthen dam to form Ratcliff Lake and planted three million seedlings to reforest the trees that had been cut down for the sawmill that once operated there. The CCC also laid roads and built a bathhouse, concession stand, and more, which are still in use today.

The large day-use area at Ratcliff Lake offers plenty of shaded green space to relax, have a picnic, and pause between jumps in the water. Loblollies and hardwoods tower above the tables and grills. A concrete path winds through the picnic area and

is a pleasant enough walk on its own, though visitors should definitely hit the national forest's many miles of hiking trails.

SWIMMING: To find the day-use area, turn off FS 520 at the picnic area and bathhouse. On the other side of the bathhouse, you'll find a sandy shore that slopes into a roped-off swim area. A wheelchair ramp runs down to the sand. Head straight into the warm, shallow water. The lake bottom is firm and sandy, and you can enjoy the forested lakeshores surrounding you. No lifeguard is on duty; swim at your own risk. This is an easily accessible swim spot in an idyllic forest.

AMENITIES: Restrooms with showers. Picnic area. Boat ramp. Wooden fishing piers. Amphitheater for rent.

PRO TIP: If time allows, take a hike along the Neches River through the Big Slough Wilderness Area inside the forest for a true experience of the area's undeveloped wilderness. (Davy Crockett cap not required.)

Tyler State Park

789 Park Road 16
Tyler, TX 75706
(903) 597-5338
tpwd.texas.gov/state-parks/tyler

HOURS: M–Th, Su 8 a.m.–5 p.m.; F 8 a.m.–9 p.m.; Sa 8 a.m.–7 p.m.

ENTRANCE FEES: $6 per adult. Free ages 12 and under. Camping fees apply.

PARK RULES: Texas Parks & Wildlife rules apply.

CAMPING: Tent, RV (water and electric hookups), screened shelters, and group facilities.

ABOUT: This wooded, well-maintained park north of Tyler, on the edge of the Pineywoods and Post Oak Savanna ecoregions, is another fine example of the work of the CCC. Architects designed the buildings in a more modern, less rustic style than those at other CCC parks. Take a moment to appreciate the sweeping view of the 64-acre lake from the bathhouse. In addition to building the bathhouse, a dance pavilion, and other features, the CCC dammed the spring-fed creek to create the lake and planted more than 600 acres of parkland with trees after farming and logging had left the land barren of native plants.

Tyler State Park offers present-day visitors a respite rich with the natural beauty of an East Texas forest. Take advantage of the many hiking trails that wind through the pine, oak, and maple trees that shade the park. Depending on the time of year, you'll catch dogwoods, azaleas, and hollies in bloom. Bring a pair of binoculars and scan the branches for a glimpse of the more than two hundred varieties of birds that live here. The plants and wildlife that live in this park are thriving thanks to the decades-long efforts of conservationists.

SWIMMING: The day-use area below the bathhouse offers a small, central sand beach and squares of unshaded grassy lawn. A concrete path runs the length of the shoreline, which stands a couple of feet above the water. Sets of stone steps with handrails provide easy access to the lake, though take care, as those steps can be slick. The swim area is buoyed off. The water, fed by nearby Beauchamp Springs, is clear and surrounded by softwood pines. A swim platform floats not far from shore. The water deepens gradually and reaches six feet or more the closer you get to the platform. No lifeguard is on duty; swim at your own risk.

AMENITIES: Restrooms with showers. Picnic area. Playground. Canoe, kayak, paddle boards, and johnboat rentals.

PRO TIP: Make sure to visit the park store here, where you'll find a well-curated inventory of souvenirs, gifts, books, snacks, and more. One of the best park stores in the state!

Central

For the purposes of this guide, Central Texas
lies west of Johnson City and extends north
to Lampasas; it includes Kerrville and the
surrounding area. (The center of the state is,
in fact, quite large, including the City of Austin
and its surrounding area, which boasts enough
natural swim spots to warrant its own section
in this guide.) The swim spots listed in this
section on Central Texas can be a bit more than
a day trip out of Austin, San Antonio, or Dallas–
Fort Worth. Kerrville is one of the best-kept
secrets in the Texas Hill Country. While Fredericksburg, Dripping Springs, and Wimberley
roll off the tips of tongues, fewer are as quick
to mention the scenic spots in Kerrville, Hunt,
Ingram, and Utopia, which offer rolling country
roads and plenty of lovely little swim holes
along the cold, emerald rivers of Central Texas.
Toss your swimsuit in an overnight bag and hit
the road for this friendly part of the state!

THE SWIMMING
HOLES OF
Central Texas

1. Badu City Park
2. Bandera City Park
3. Black Rock Park
4. Boerne City Lake Park
5. Cypress Bend Park
6. Flat Rock Park
7. Guadalupe River State Park
8. Hancock Springs Free Flow Pool
9. Ingram Dam
10. Inks Lake State Park
11. James Kiehl River Bend Park
12. Kerrville-Schreiner Park
13. Lions Park
14. Llano River Slab
15. Louise Hays Park
16. Moffett Park
17. Pedernales Falls State Park
18. Robinson Llano County Park
19. Schumacher Crossing
20. Wagon Wheel Crossing

Badu City Park

300 Legion Drive
Llano, TX 78643
(352) 247-78643
cityofllano.com/facilities/facility/details/
Badu-City-Park-3

HOURS: Check posted signs for current hours.
ENTRANCE FEES: Free. Camping fees apply.
PARK RULES: Llano City rules apply. Obey all posted signs.
CAMPING: RV camping (water and electric hookups) only.
ABOUT: This city park is a nice, scenic place to stop for a quick

dip, a picnic, and a few souvenir photos of downtown Llano. Inks Bridge spans a stretch of the Llano River where it's impounded by the Llano River Dam. A long grassy area offers room for recreation, and a walkway traces the river's edge. This is a simple, straightforward park with a terrific view of Llano and a pretty view of the water crashing over the dam and onto boulders and the riverbed below.

SWIMMING: The water is accessible just above the dam wall from a small, sand-and-grass bank that ends in a long shelf of concrete steps that descend into the pretty, blue, clear water. Diving is not permitted as the water is quite shallow. This is a great spot for kids to do a bit of easy swimming, though do be aware that the river's current can grab swimmers farther from shore.

AMENITIES: Restroom. Picnic tables with grills. Pavilion. Playground. Basketball Court.

PRO TIP: Check out Fuel Coffee Shop on East Main Street in Llano, which in addition to brewing up a great cup of coffee regularly hosts live music and other community events.

Bandera City Park

1102 Maple Street
Bandera, TX 78003
(830) 796-3765
cityofbandera.org/2161/park

HOURS: 8 a.m. to dusk.
ENTRANCE FEES: M–F free. Sa–Su $5.00 per adult (March–Oct). Free ages 3 and under.
PARK RULES: Glass containers, swimming near or standing on the dam, open fires, and loud music prohibited.
CAMPING: Not available.
ABOUT: Right off Main Street in bustling, tourist-friendly downtown Bandera you'll find Bandera City Park, 77 acres of cypress-rich green land flanking a stretch of the Medina River that's prime for swimming. Plenty of picnic tables, barbecue

grills, and playground equipment make this a comfortable, easy spot to spend a day with the family. Kayaking and rafting are available. This is a great spot to dog-watch. If you bring your dog, make sure to keep your pal on leash. Hop on the River Bend Native Plant Trail and enjoy the sights of sycamores, live oaks, and more. Bandera is also a popular spot for birders, and the park is part of the Heart of Texas Wildlife Trail. Catch the city's annual riverfest in the summer.

SWIMMING: The spring-fed Medina River is particularly lovely at this location when the rain has been good and the water is high. Be aware that the hot summer months can dry out the Medina; call ahead to check swim conditions before heading out. The water is a remarkable sparkling jade color, and the long stretch of riverbank offers plenty of access off cypress knees, grassy banks, and a rope swing. Some points along the bank are lower and offer easier entry than others. The river is narrow within the park, and swimmers can easily make their way from one side of the crystal-clear, limestone-bottomed river to the other. No lifeguard is on duty; swim at your own risk.

AMENITIES: Picnic area with grills. Volleyball court. Disc golf. Bird observation area and butterfly garden.

PRO TIP: Bandera dubs itself the "Cowboy Capital of the World"; during the late nineteenth century the town was the start of the Great Western Cattle Trail. Popular with bikers and antique hunters alike, Bandera prides itself on its old-time Texas aesthetic, traditions, and values.

CENTRAL

Black Rock Park

3400 State Highway 261
Buchanan Dam, TX 78609
(512) 369-4774
lcra.org/parks/Pages /black-rock-park.aspx

HOURS: Dawn to dusk.

ENTRANCE FEES: $5 per adult. Free ages 12 and under. $2 for disabled and seniors 65 and older. Camping fees apply.

PARK RULES: Glass containers and public consumption or display of alcoholic beverages prohibited. Pets must be on leash.

CAMPING: Tent, RV (water and electric hookups), and air-conditioned cabins. Spots are spacious.

ABOUT: Black Rock Park is a terrific 25-acre spot on the west shore of Lake Buchanan. It offers clean, modern amenities, plenty of room for camping, and a long shoreline that provides easy access to lake swimming. This is a good family spot with lots of space to get into the water.

Lake Buchanan is the first of the Highland Lakes, a series of impoundments on the Colorado River, and is now maintained by the Lower Colorado River Authority (LCRA). With eighteen air-conditioned mini cabins, dozens of RV hookups, and spacious and shaded tent camping, Black Rock Park is a comfortable spot for an overnight getaway. Early reservations are recommended. The roads here are wide and paved and the sites are well maintained.

SWIMMING: Day use is welcome from dawn to dusk. There's plenty of room on the wide, grassy bank to set up for the day. The immediate shoreline is sandy and slopes directly into the water. This is a popular spot to bring a tube and float. Be prepared to meet a large crowd on summer weekends. No lifeguard is on duty; swim at your own risk.

AMENITIES: Restrooms with showers. Picnic area with grills.
PRO TIP: This is a good spot for families. Be sure to bring your own shade, as there's not much available here.

Boerne City Lake Park

1 City Lake Road
Boerne, TX 78006
(830) 249-9511
ci.boerne.tx.us/169/City-Lake-Park

HOURS: 5 a.m.–10 p.m.

ENTRANCE FEES: M–Th $10 parking fee, F–Su $15. $5 parking fee for disabled, 65 and older, and all active or retired military. Free for City of Boerne residents.

PARK RULES: Glass containers, firearms, swimming or wading within fifty feet of the boat ramp prohibited. Fires in grills and fire pits only. Pets must be on leash.

CAMPING: Not available.

ABOUT: Scenic City Lake Park in Boerne is a picture-postcard spot for swimming in Central Texas. Located approximately forty minutes northwest of San Antonio, the lake is the result of

a city initiative in the early 1970s that dammed Cibolo Creek as a means of flood control. Boerne Lake is a huge, beautiful stretch of blue water accessible via a well-maintained park that was developed by the city in 2005. The view from all sides of the park is impressive. Here at City Lake Park you'll feel removed from town life and immersed in the natural beauty of Central Texas. You'll also appreciate the rare opportunity to swim in a Texas lake kept quiet and still by the prohibition of motorized boats.

SWIMMING: The ample, beachlike shoreline allows for multiple points of entry to the calm waters of Boerne Lake. The park's wide green lawn slopes down to the shore, where you can wade up to your ankles in shallow water or wander deeper to swim. The gentle entry into the lake makes this an ideal spot for family swimming or for anyone who would benefit from easy access to the water.

AMENITIES: Picnic area with grills. Volleyball court. Disc golf. Bird observation area and butterfly garden.

PRO TIP: It's pronounced "BURN-ee."

Cypress Bend Park

503 Peace Avenue
New Braunfels, TX 78130
(830) 221-4350
nbtexas.org/1672/Cypress-Bend-Park

HOURS: 10 a.m.–7 p.m.
ENTRANCE FEES: Free.
PARK RULES: Glass, Styrofoam, and jumping from trees into the water prohibited. Alcohol is permitted; volume drinking devices (e.g., kegs) prohibited. Coolers must have locking mechanism.
CAMPING: Not available.

ABOUT: Just down the road from Schlitterbahn New Braunfels Waterpark is a spacious, well-maintained park that offers plenty of access to the Guadalupe River. Cypress Bend is a tucked away, 15-acre park known for its wide, long stretch of open lawn that's rarely crowded. The space for running around makes this a good spot to bring a family. While bald cypresses grow along the water's edge, note that the lawn here is unshaded. If a hectic day at Schlitterbahn isn't on your bucket list, skip the busy water park and head to this calm, quiet spot in New Braunfels instead.

SWIMMING: Access to the water is available from the riverbank. Depending on the current water level and where you decide to get in, you can either step down over bald cypress roots and an uneven bank to get into the water, or you can find a spot where the bank eases right into the river. Water levels do vary, with some deeper spots for swimming and shallow spots for wading. The bottom is sandy here. This is easy, pleasant swimming in a pretty stretch of the Guadalupe. No lifeguard is on duty; swim at your own risk.

AMENITIES: Restrooms. Picnic areas with grills. Playground. Pavilion. Horseshoe pit.

PRO TIP: Take a stroll through historic, visitor-friendly New Braunfels after your swim. It has long been a pretty, popular tourist spot in Central Texas.

Flat Rock Park

3840 Riverside Drive
Kerrville, TX 78028
(830) 257-7300
co.kerr.tx.us/facilities

HOURS: Dawn to dusk.

ENTRANCE FEES: $4 per adult. $1 per child. $2 per senior. $10 per carload maximum.

PARK RULES: Pets are permitted.

CAMPING: Not available.

ABOUT: Flat Rock Park, also known as Flat Rock Lake Park, offers basic access to the Guadalupe River on Kerrville's east side. The volume of open space here is what makes Flat Rock Park stand out. With fewer bells and whistles than Kerrville's Louise Hays Park, Flat Rock boasts a large stretch of flat, grassy land with plenty of shade trees just across the water from Kerrville-Schreiner Park. This is a popular spot for fishing and boat access and an easy place to bring the whole family.

SWIMMING: Drive right up to the water's edge and park. Bald cypresses grow along the riverbank, providing several good spots to leverage their roots as steps into the water. A rocky riverbed makes swim shoes a good idea. No lifeguard is on duty; swim at your own risk. Water depth will vary depending on recent rainfall, though this is typically a reliable part of the Guadalupe in which to immerse yourself and go for a good swim.

AMENITIES: Picnic tables. Boat ramp. Otherwise, amenities are limited.

PRO TIP: Bring your pup to run around. This is the only off-leash park in the area.

Guadalupe River State Park

3350 Park Road 31
Spring Branch, TX 78070
(830) 438-2656
tpwd.texas.gov/state-parks/guadalupe-river

HOURS: 8 a.m.–10 p.m.
ENTRANCE FEES: $7 per adult. Free ages 12 and under. Camping fees apply.
PARK RULES: Texas Parks & Wildlife rules apply.
CAMPING: Tent and RV (water and electric hookups).
ABOUT: Thirty miles north of downtown San Antonio,

Guadalupe River State Park encompasses nearly 2,000 acres of some of the most beautiful natural land the Texas Hill Country has to offer. First opened to the public in 1983, the park offers campsites, fishing, equestrian trails, and several miles of walking and biking trails. Hike to the discovery center for interactive nature exhibits. Check out Swallow Cliff in spring and early summer to view a colony of cliff swallows.

While this is one of the most naturally beautiful places to spend a swim day in Central Texas, it is wild terrain. The river isn't dammed here, and swimmers are advised to mind the current, which can change swiftly and unexpectedly. Watch out for rocks, drop-offs, eddies, and debris.

SWIMMING: The Guadalupe River cuts through the center of the park and offers four miles of accessible riverfront. A series of stone steps with wooden handrails leads down from the paved parking lot to a long gravel path where you'll find picnic tables. From there, head down to the pebbled bank of the Guadalupe. This is a highly popular swim destination. Bring your floats, tubes, coolers, and sunblock and enjoy swimming against the backdrop of the beautiful limestone cliff face cut by the river. No lifeguard is on duty; swim at your own risk.

AMENITIES: Restrooms with showers. Picnic area with grills. Park store. Playground. Pavilion.

PRO TIP: While you're in the region, take a guided tour of nearby Honey Creek State Natural Area, a 2,300-acre area frequented by humans since early hunter-gatherers roamed Central Texas. Entry is by guided tour only. To see the tour schedule, visit honeycreekfriends.org.

Hancock Springs Free Flow Pool

Hancock Park Highway, US 281
Lampasas, TX 76550
(512) 556-4048
lampasas.org/157/swimming-pool

HOURS: Th–Sa 12 p.m.–7 p.m., Su 1 p.m.–6 p.m. (M–W closed).
ENTRANCE FEES: $3.50 per adult. $2.50 ages 3–12 and seniors 62 and older. Free ages 0–2.
PARK RULES: Children ages 8 and under must be accompanied by an adult. Outside food and drink are allowed. See full rules at park entrance.
CAMPING: Not available.
ABOUT: Located on Sulphur Creek in Lampasas, Hancock Free Flow Pool in Hancock Park is one of the oldest spring-fed swimming pools in Texas. The springs were popularized in the 1850s when Hanna Hughes, a member of the first family to settle the area, was deemed cured of her ailments by the spring's restorative powers. Word spread, and by the 1880s the springs were billed as a health resort, a veritable "Saratoga of the South." The swimming pool was built around the springs in 1911 by the Baptist Encampment for Central Texans. The city bought the property in 1936. During World War II it was leased to Camp Hood and known as "Panther Park," a place for soldiers to convalesce and enjoy a bit of recreation.

Located alongside the pool is the Hostess House, originally built by the Baptist Encampment. Over the years it has been used for dances, performances, and entertainment; it was eventually restored by the Daughters of the Republic of Texas. Stop by the historical marker on your way in from the parking lot to read more of the story. Hancock Springs Free Flow Pool is a clean, easy, well-maintained place to refresh and experience a little bit of Central Texas history.

SWIMMING: The water at Hancock is clear and cold, a steady 69° all year long. A concrete embankment surrounds the pool and ladders lead down into the water. The pool is roped off into three sections and has a shallow and a deep end. Mineral-rich water flows through the pool and out again to feed Sulphur Creek. Occasionally, the water smells like sulphur; this is a naturally occurring, untreated swim spot. Lifeguards are on duty.

AMENITIES: Picnic tables. Clean, modern restrooms and changing facilities available in the Hostess House.

PRO TIP: Hancock is closed more often than it's open. Be sure to double-check the pool's hours before heading down.

Ingram Dam

610 TX-39
Ingram, TX 78025

HOURS: Open daily.

ENTRANCE FEES: Free.

PARK RULES: "Respect the river . . . it is far more powerful than you are!"

CAMPING: Not available.

ABOUT: One of the most popular water spots in the Kerrville area is the Ingram Dam, located in the town of Ingram on Highway 39 between Hunt and Kerrville. Built in 1954 as an upgrade

in flood control from the "Old Ingram Dam," the dam impounds the Guadalupe River at a point where its southern bank rises up to a picturesque low hill lined with native trees. The big activity at Ingram Dam is dam sliding. In tubes, kayaks, and on their own, locals send themselves sliding down the long, algae-slick concrete dam into a pooled portion of river. Ropes slung down the side help you climb back up to the top and do it all over again.

SWIMMING: The water above the dam is quite deep. Children should wear life jackets, and all swimmers should be aware that river depth and currents vary. Be aware of any logs or debris the river may be carrying. The long, narrow dam wall is a spot for sunbathing and dangling your feet in the water. Concrete steps lead into the river at a few points along the dam wall. No lifeguard is on duty; swim at your own risk.

AMENITIES: Parking is available across the narrow highway.

PRO TIP: If you're game to try out dam sliding with the locals, consider bringing a tube or some sort of padding for protection.

CENTRAL

Inks Lake State Park

3630 Park Road 4 West
Burnet, TX 78611
(512) 793-2223
tpwd.texas.gov/state-parks/inks-lake

HOURS: 7 a.m.–10 p.m.

ENTRANCE FEES: $6 per adult. Free ages 12 and under. Camping fees apply.

PARK RULES: Texas Parks & Wildlife rules apply.

CAMPING: Tent, RV (water and electric hookups), screened shelters, and group facilities.

ABOUT: Inks Lake State Park sits near Burnet at the southeastern end of Inks Lake, the second of the six Highland Lakes built on the Colorado River for flood control. The park was originally a project of the CCC; after completing park facilities for nearby Longhorn Cavern and constructing surrounding roads, the unit turned to work on Inks Lake Park. The project was completed by the State Parks Board, which opened Inks Lake Park in 1950. Today Inks Lake is a popular overnight camping destination, boasting over two hundred campsites for tents and RVs and twenty-two cabins. Many sites have lake access. With nine miles of hiking trails and swimming available, day use is also welcome.

SWIMMING: The most popular spot for day-use swimming at Inks Lake is Devil's Waterhole. Given the busy campsites that wind through the park, Devil's Waterhole can be a bit tricky to find. Be sure to pick up a map at the park ranger's office or print one from the Texas Parks & Wildlife website. Follow signs for campsites numbered in the mid-200s. Signs along the road are low to the ground, and there aren't many for Devil's Waterhole. You'll drive through several campsites and end up in a parking area at the top of Devil's Waterhole Trail. From here it's a short, flat walk to Devil's Waterhole. A sign with safe swimming

recommendations lets you know you've arrived. The water here is quite deep. Floatation devices are highly recommended for young swimmers to safely enjoy the water. Access from the banks is a bit steep. The primary way people enjoy Devil's Hole is by jumping from the low surrounding cliffs. No lifeguard is on duty; swim at your own risk.

AMENITIES: Modern restrooms with showers. Picnic areas. Park store. Playground. Boat rentals.

PRO TIP: If cliff-diving and deepwater floating don't appeal, check out Valley Spring Trail. Hike up billion-year-old gneiss rock and take the three-quarter-mile loop. When the creek is running, you'll find falls tumbling over ancient pink and grey rock.

James Kiehl River Bend Park

118 River Bend Road
Comfort, TX 78013
kendallcountyparks.org

HOURS: 7 a.m. to dusk.

ENTRANCE FEES: Free.

PARK RULES: All Texas state wildlife and boating laws apply.
Glass containers, Styrofoam, motorized boats, public display of
alcoholic beverages, and ground fires prohibited. Minors must
be accompanied by an adult. Pets must be on leash.

CAMPING: Not available.

ABOUT: Here in rural Comfort, past the rusted trestle of the
defunct Fredericksburg railroad and nestled in deep pastoral
quiet, you'll find a 25-acre park developed in memory of a local
young veteran, James Kiehl, who enlisted in the US Army and

was sent to Iraq in 2003 to repair computers and fiber-optic cables. His convoy was ambushed in March 2003 in Ah Nasariah. James's story, along with a sandstone monument dedicated to all Kendall County servicemen and -women, can be found in the Memorial Grove beside the parking area.

With 1,634 feet of river frontage, this is a simple, pretty place to swim and settle in the shade and sun. It's a bit of a drive to get out here, so families with restless kids who might be looking for a little more to do than splash and poke around might want to consider plans before making the trip. Hiking trails are available, including the Pecan Loop, which takes you along the old San Antonio and Aransas Pass rail bed. Bring your own water; there's no potable water available.

SWIMMING: The swimming hole itself is accessible via a sloping dirt path that takes you over a bank of sun-bleached rocks to a concrete bridge. Wear good shoes to hike this short trail; flip-flops are not recommended. On the other side of this rocky slope, you'll find an enchanting piece of the Guadalupe River babbling over rocks and bald cypress roots, ideal for sitting and soaking. This small, secluded space shaded by tall cypress trees feels like a little piece of magic in the middle of nowhere. The natural landscape is entirely preserved. No lifeguard is on duty; swim at your own risk.

AMENITIES: Latrine bathroom. Benches available in Memorial Grove. No potable water.

PRO TIP: On your way out, take a drive by the nearby Brownsboro Cemetery, established in 1870. The Brownsboro community was settled by shingle-makers in the mid-1800s. The parkland was once part of this community. If you're interested in local history, take a slow turn through Comfort and watch for the many original buildings still standing in town.

CENTRAL

Kerrville-Schreiner Park

2385 Bandera Highway
Kerrville, TX 78028
(830) 257-5392
kerrvilletx.gov/318/Kerville-Schreiner-Park

HOURS: 8 a.m.–10 p.m.

ENTRANCE FEES: $6 per adult. $2 per senior and ages 12 and under. $10 per carload maximum. Camping fees apply.

PARK RULES: Pets must be on leash and are not permitted in the swim/river area.

CAMPING: Tent, RV (water and electric hookups), and cabins.

ABOUT: Kerrville-Schreiner Park is a 517-acre developed city park replete with miles of hiking trails, campsites, RV camping, a butterfly garden, and many amenities. Be aware that this is a very popular park; during peak times and seasons, expect to see a line of cars waiting at the entrance. The CCC developed the park in the late 1930s after the City of Kerrville donated the acreage to the State Parks Board in 1934. If you check out the old plans via the Texas State Library and Archives Commission, you'll see a sketch for a proposed amusement park. The park was returned to Kerrville in 2004 under an act that saw several parks across Texas transferred from state ownership to local city governance. The move allowed for many much-needed repairs and improvements to be made.

SWIMMING: Swimmers can purchase a day pass and head to a stretch of shady bank along the Guadalupe. The water is easily accessible from the riverbank, and the riverbed is a bit rocky. Live oaks and Spanish oaks line the banks and offer ample shade. Pull up a blanket or stake out a seat at one of the many nearby picnic tables.

AMENITIES: Restrooms. Picnic areas with barbecue pits. Basketball courts. Boat ramp. Pavilions. Playground. Hiking trails.

PRO TIP: To make the most of this park, take advantage of the many activities and amenities available. For swimming alone, other local spots may prove more rewarding for day use.

Lions Park

300 Lions Park Road
Center Point, TX 78010

HOURS: Open daily.
ENTRANCE FEES: Free.
PARK RULES: Texas state wildlife and boating laws apply.
CAMPING: Not available.
ABOUT: In the small town of Center Point, southeast of Kerrville on the Guadalupe River, you'll find signs pointing the way toward Lions Park, a nice little spot along Center Point Lake you might not find with GPS. Here the Center Point Lake Dam creates a serene swimming hole at a low-water crossing. You won't encounter any formal welcome signs when you arrive,

just a circular dirt path, a few picnic benches, and, to the back, a couple of basketball hoops and a volleyball net. There is some basic development, including a set of concrete steps built down to the water above the dam.

SWIMMING: The dam is not too high. Easy access is available both to the still waters above the dam and to the area below the falls, where you can watch the water rush beneath the crossing on its way southeast. Take care with your footing, as the rocky embankment below the dam is quite slippery. No lifeguard is on duty; swim at your own risk.

AMENITIES: Portable toilets. Bring your own water.

PRO TIP: Center Point is a quintessentially small, quiet Texas town, with several churches, a Family Dollar, and a Dollar General. Pack a lunch or plan to either pick up provisions or dine out in nearby Kerrville.

Llano River Slab

**Llano River at FM 3404/Slab Road
Kingsland, TX 78639**

HOURS: Natural, undeveloped swim spot. Swimming dependent on weather and water levels.

ENTRANCE FEES: Free.

PARK RULES: Not part of a park system.

CAMPING: Not available.

ABOUT: Out on FM 3404 in Kingsland, just over a mile west of FM 1431, a low-water crossing of the Llano River has created one of the most popular unofficial swimming holes west of Austin. Known to locals as either Slab Road, Kingsland Slab, or Llano River Slab, this particularly picturesque stretch of undeveloped pink granite draws hundreds of visitors who enjoy the natural landscape on a hot, sunny day.

SWIMMING: Water levels here are heavily dependent on rainfall. In ideal conditions, swimming is possible on either side of the crossing. The west bank typically provides a wider swimming hole with a soft bottom. To the east, dips and pockets of various sizes in the granite fill with water and create shallow wading areas (sometimes quite sizable) for kids, and they offer an easy place to set up a chair and dip in your feet. It's not unusual to see inflatable tubes, beach chairs, and typical swim gear here. Fishing isn't permitted, which makes this spot particularly attractive, as you don't have to contend with fishing line. Swim at your own risk.

AMENITIES: Park along the side of the road just west of the crossing. Watch for traffic when entering and exiting your vehicle. As mentioned above, this site is undeveloped, so there are no restroom facilities or amenities of any kind. Bring your own drinking water. Local law enforcement does monitor activity

here on busy days; however, there's no regular supervision or explicitly enforced rules. People do bring dogs here.

PRO TIP: The granite gets dangerously hot during the blistering summer months. Protect your feet and those of your pets.

Louise Hays Park

202 Thompson Drive
Kerrville, TX 78028
(830) 257-7300
kerrvilletx.gov/829/Louise-Hays-Park

HOURS: Dawn to 11 p.m.
ENTRANCE FEES: Free.
PARK RULES: Smoking, sleeping, overnight camping, ground fires, glass containers, and firearms prohibited. Jumping into the water from dams, bridges, trees, and streets prohibited. Pets must be on leash.

CAMPING: Not available.

ABOUT: In the heart of Kerrville on the Guadalupe River is an enormous, well-tended, beautiful city park, a 63.5-acre project that was all built in a single day! In 1950 Kerrville resident Robert Hays donated 35 acres of riverfront property to the city of Kerrville to build a public park. There were two conditions: first, that the park be named for Louise Hays, Robert's wife; and second, that the park be built in one day. The city agreed. At 7 a.m. on April 25, 1950, a crew of virtually every able-bodied man in town, totaling more than one thousand volunteers, set to work. By the end of the day, Kerrville had a park.

There is much to enjoy on the expansive grounds of Louise Hays Park. Walk the footbridge to Tranquility Island or take the wooden staircase up to the garden and play area behind Butt-Holdsworth Memorial Library. Get some exercise at the sand volleyball court, hang out at the dog park, enjoy a snack at one of the many picnic areas, or take the kids to the splash pad. You'll find a large commercial barbecue pit, two pavilions available for rent, basketball courts, and plenty of grass to spread out, relax, and take it all in.

SWIMMING: Louise Hays Park offers plentiful access to the Guadalupe River. Enter between trees growing along the bank, or walk toward the dam for prime spots to step in for a swim off concrete embankments. Keep an eye out for turtles sunning themselves on the roots of cypress trees. This is an easy, comfortable place to enjoy the blue-green waters of the Guadalupe.

AMENITIES: Clean and modern restrooms with showers. Picnic areas. Volleyball court. Dog park.

PRO TIP: Louise Hays Park is a key part of the Kerrville River Trail, a four-mile, paved public walking and biking trail that connects Kerrville-Shreiner Park, Louise Hays Park, Lehmann-Monroe Park, the Riverside Nature Center, and Lowry Park. Make time to take a hike!

CENTRAL

Moffett Park

County Road Crossing
State Highway 16
Medina, TX 78055

HOURS: Open daily.

ENTRANCE FEES: Free.

PARK RULES: Overnight camping, loud music after 10 p.m., and fireworks prohibited.

CAMPING: Not available.

ABOUT: On the west side of the town of Medina, off the beaten path between the town and private ranchland, is secluded Moffett Park. You won't find this one with GPS. Head down Patterson Avenue off Route 16 and you'll come to this hidden gem that boasts a beautiful view of big skies and open land. Though you're not far from houses and a residential area, you'll easily feel as though you're in the middle of nowhere. The only amenity you'll find is the peace and calm of unaltered nature.

SWIMMING: Walk right into the shallow, crystal-clear water of the Medina River from the grassy, tree-lined bank. The Medina is narrow here and the bank undeveloped. Swimming is dependent on water levels. This is a beautiful place to sit and relax rather than jump in for a serious swim. No lifeguard is on duty; swim at your own risk.

AMENITIES: There are no restroom facilities or amenities of any kind. Bring your own drinking water.

PRO TIP: Just getting here is all the tip you need. Use your old-school map skills; GPS won't get you here.

Pedernales Falls State Park

> 2585 Park Road 6026
> Johnson City, TX 78636
> (830) 868-7304
> tpwd.texas.gov/state-parks/pedernales-falls

HOURS: 8 a.m.–10 p.m.

ENTRANCE FEES: $6 per adult. Free ages 12 and under. Camping fees apply.

PARK RULES: Texas Parks & Wildlife rules apply.

CAMPING: Primitive, tent, equestrian, and RV (water and electric hookups).

ABOUT: Pedernales ("Per-deh-NAL-es," according to Lyndon B. Johnson) Falls State Park is a beautiful park located approximately thirty miles west of Austin, just northwest of Dripping Springs in the rolling Texas Hill Country. Pedernales is famous for its falls, where clear water rushes over a series of naturally occurring steps of three-hundred-million-year-old river limestone. Smooth river rocks, plenty of shade, and an ever-flowing river make this a tranquil, soothing place to visit.

This is a popular spot for campers. When the park hits capacity, it will close to anyone without overnight camping reservations.

SWIMMING: From the day-use parking lot, walk down a gravel path to an overlook that gives you a lovely view of the river. A long flight of stone steps leads down to the sandy banks. This is the only way to get down to the swimmable portion of the river. Traversing the stairs with a heavy pack or picnic basket can be strenuous. Keep the steps in mind when you're packing your load for the day. Keep it light.

The constantly flowing river is temperate and never too cold. Smooth river stones line the riverbed, which is rimmed by large boulders along the banks. Prop yourself up against one of the boulders and let the Pedernales flow around you, or spread a blanket on the beachlike bank of thick sand. Keep in mind that the sand can be quite hot in the summer, so take care of the sensitive feet of your pets and yourself. The riverbanks are lined with bald cypress and sycamore trees.

The river is prone to flash flooding. Be sure to read all posted signage. A flooded river is serious business. Heed all park warnings and mind the weather. If the river starts to rise and the water turns muddy, seek higher ground.

AMENITIES: Restrooms. Picnic area with grills. Park store. Hike, bike, and equestrian trails.

PRO TIP: Be sure to check out the falls from the overlook on the north side of the park. The water temperature tends to be a little warm, so visiting for a swim in spring and fall is a good plan. Note: During the peak summer months, once capacity is reached this popular park will close to visitors without overnight camping permits; it will reopen when there's room in the parking lot.

Robinson Llano County Park

Texas Highway 16 and FM 152
Llano, TX 78643
(325) 247-4158
cityofllano.com/Facilities/Facility/Details/
Robinson-City-Park-2

HOURS: M–F 6 a.m. to midnight; Sa 6 a.m.–1 a.m. (Su).
ENTRANCE FEES: Free. Camping fees apply.
PARK RULES: Consumption of alcoholic beverages permitted during regular hours only. Discharging firearms prohibited.
CAMPING: Tent and RV.

ABOUT: Approximately two miles west of downtown Llano is Robinson Llano County Park, a calm, shaded spot to dip into the impounded Llano River. Turn right on Norton Drive when you enter the park and head past the RV and tent sites and a long, grassy area to a small parking lot near the short dam wall.

SWIMMING: Robinson City Park offers a long stretch of frontage to Llano Park Lake, and plenty of trees shade the wide, grassy bank. Easy access to the water is available above the dam wall. The water gets deep here, but it's shallow enough just near the dam. The bottom is soft. Swim down a bit, turn your back to the wall, and enjoy the impressive view of the Llano River.

AMENITIES: Restrooms with showers. Picnic area with grills. Basketball court. Hike and bike trails. Playground. Potable water. Horseback riding.

PRO TIP: Head into Llano after your swim and spend some time touring the shops and historic buildings of small-town Llano.

CENTRAL

Schumacher Crossing

| State Highway 39, between Hunt and Ingram
| Hunt, TX 78024

HOURS: Natural, undeveloped swim spot. Swimming is dependent on weather and water levels.

ENTRANCE FEES: Free.

PARK RULES: Not part of a park system.

CAMPING: Not available.

ABOUT: East of Hunt and a close shot from Kerrville down State Highway 39 is a popular side-of-the-road swim spot known as Schumacher Crossing. You'll find a simple setup here: small parking lot, covered picnic table, single grill, and, below the modern paved road, the original concrete crossing hand-poured by a county crew in the 1920s. Take a moment to spot, in the concrete, the name of the crew's foreman, who proudly declared the site, "Made by Otto Mayer, July 25th 1929." The crossing is named for Christian Schumacher, who emigrated with his family from Germany in 1845 and settled the land behind the crossing. A historical marker was dedicated there in 2002 to commemorate the Schumachers' work and impact on the area, which includes a road between Hunt and Ingram that opened Hunt to tourism.

SWIMMING: Head down the short concrete slope from the parking lot to the water. This small pocket of the Guadalupe is the result of dams built by the Schumacher sons in the early 1920s. Step over tree roots and a rocky, vegetated bank to access the water here. Water depth varies. This spot is well known and fills up quickly on warm weekends. Swim at your own risk.

AMENITIES: Restrooms are not available.

PRO TIP: If you hit Schumacher and find it packed, continue up the road to Hunt, where plenty more swim opportunities await.

Wagon Wheel Crossing

FM 1340
Hunt, TX 78024

HOURS: Natural, undeveloped swim spot. Swimming is dependent on weather and water levels.

ENTRANCE FEES: Free.

PARK RULES: Not part of a park system.

CAMPING: Not available.

ABOUT: Turn west down FM 1340 at the Hunt General Store and take a drive down a scenic, curving road that crosses the Guadalupe River at several points. You'll find many spots to pull over, park on the side of the road, and take a dip. About eight miles down from the general store is a spot favored by locals, Wagon Wheel Crossing.

This is a crossing, not a formal swim spot. There is no parking lot or development whatsoever, which is the charm and beauty of this particular swimming hole; it's easy and accessible, yet it feels remote and undiscovered. Take care when parking your vehicle on the side of the road: there is space to do it safely, but this is a country road traversed by plenty of pickups and other vehicles. Step off the road onto the limestone embankment that makes Wagon Wheel Crossing the attractive spot that it is. The rocks are perfect for lounging and picnicking. Bring a blanket or chairs and post up for a pleasant day.

SWIMMING: This is a small spot with shallow water that's good for wading. The short falls on the south side of the road are attractive, but pay attention to the "No Trespassing" signs that mark the surrounding area. Stick to the limestone bank and slow current on the north side of the crossing for a peaceful swim. Swim at your own risk.

AMENITIES: No restroom facilities or amenities of any kind. Bring your own drinking water.

PRO TIP: If you find Wagon Wheel Crossing full on a hot summer day, head on down 1340 about half a mile and keep your eyes peeled for the Flats at Benson Crossing. While the water here isn't quite deep enough to swim, underwater rock formations make it an easy place to sit and cool off. Head back in the other direction toward the intersection of FM 1340 and Highway 39 and you'll hit Hunt Crossing, where the bridge spans a popular swimming hole with a rope swing.

Austin

AND THE SURROUNDING AREA

If you know Austin, you know Barton Springs. You know Hamilton Pool and Lake Travis and maybe Blue Hole Wimberley and the milky jade of the San Marcos River. But have you posed with the bluebonnets at Muleshoe? Have you walked on ancient lava at McKinney Falls? Have you swung on the rope swing at William & Eleanor Crook Park? Did you know there's yet another Blue Hole up in Georgetown? Austin and its surrounding towns are waiting to be explored. As the population rises in the Capital City and the line to get into Barton Springs stretches closer and closer to the Frost Bank Tower every day, make an effort to expand your horizons and discover what lies just beyond the city. This part of the Edwards Aquifer boasts an extraordinary number of natural springs (Hello, Krause) that support a unique ecological environment. (Hello, everyone who must work to preserve the Barton Creek Greenbelt—this includes you.) Grab a tube, find a spot on one of the many waterways, and enjoy all this bustling area has to offer.

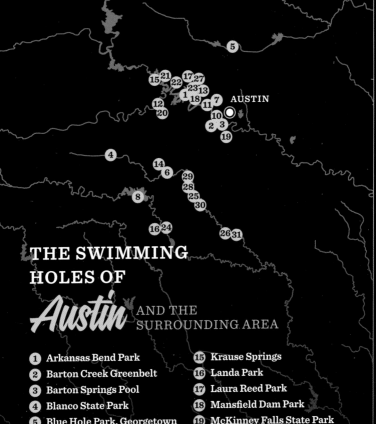

THE SWIMMING HOLES OF

Austin AND THE SURROUNDING AREA

1. Arkansas Bend Park
2. Barton Creek Greenbelt
3. Barton Springs Pool
4. Blanco State Park
5. Blue Hole Park, Georgetown
6. Blue Hole Regional Park, Wimberley
7. Bull Creek District Park
8. Canyon Lake Park
9. Colorado Bend State Park
10. Deep Eddy Pool
11. Emma Long Metropolitan Park
12. Hamilton Pool Preserve
13. Hippie Hollow/McGregor County Park
14. Jacob's Well Natural Area

15. Krause Springs
16. Landa Park
17. Laura Reed Park
18. Mansfield Dam Park
19. McKinney Falls State Park
20. Milton Reimers Ranch
21. Muleshoe Bend Recreation Area
22. Pace Bend Park
23. The Point at Bob Wentz Park
24. Prince Solms Park
25. Rio Vista Park
26. River Trail Park
27. Sandy Creek Park
28. San Marcos City Park
29. Sewell Park
30. William & Eleanor Crook Park
31. Zedler Mill Park South

Arkansas Bend Park

16900 Cherry Lane
Lago Vista, TX 78645
(512) 854-7275
parks.traviscountytx.gov/parks/arkansas-bend

HOURS: Dawn to dusk.

ENTRANCE FEES: $10 per vehicle. $3 per pedestrian or cyclist. Free for seniors 62 and older and for Lone Star veterans. Cash or check only; credit and debit cards not accepted. Camping fees apply.

PARK RULES: Glass containers, public display of alcohol, tobacco products, and firearms prohibited. Pets must be on leash.

CAMPING: Campsites with picnic tables and restrooms. Reservations available online. Quiet hours enforced 10 p.m.–7 a.m.

ABOUT: Nestled on Lake Travis's quieter north shore, Arkansas Bend Park is notable for its rocky, beachlike shoreline, smaller crowds, and the coves and inlets waiting to be explored. This 323-acre park is a serene, picturesque Central Texas gem and is well worth the drive north of the lake. A bluff overlooking the water is a fine place to settle in for a picnic at one of the shaded tables and a popular place for campers to pitch a tent. While adventurous swimmers might find it tempting to launch into the water from some of the park's rocky heights, be aware that there are many large rocks beneath the water's surface along the shoreline that make jumping particularly dangerous. Arkansas Bend's distance from the frequented swim spots closer to Austin make for a more natural, low-key swim experience.

SWIMMING: Two miles of shoreline offer plenty of opportunities to get into the water. Three fingers of land extend into the lake; the middle is most popular for swimming. The sandy, rocky shoreline slopes into the lake at a soft, easy angle. The water at Arkansas Bend is a remarkable emerald color, enhancing the beachlike quality of the experience. Bring a tube or simply wade in—this spot is easy to enjoy.

AMENITIES: Shaded picnic tables with grills. Boat ramp. Bathrooms. Hiking. Fishing.

PRO TIP: If you plan to camp, make sure you bring water and charge your devices before pitching your tent. Only primitive camping is available here.

Barton Creek Greenbelt

austinparks.org

HOURS: Open daily. Austin park curfew is 10 p.m.
ENTRANCE FEES: Free.
PARK RULES: Restrictions are clearly posted at the trailheads. Camping, smoking, alcohol, and glass prohibited. Pets must be on leash.
CAMPING: Not available.
ABOUT: The Barton Creek Greenbelt, seven and a quarter miles of protected land located along the curving center of Austin's Barton Creek, is where Austinites go to swim, hike, and relieve themselves of condos, bars, MoPac traffic, and festival mayhem. With its headwaters in Hays County, Barton Creek flows forty miles east to the Colorado River (Lady Bird Lake) in downtown Austin. The creek is home to a wide variety of plants and wildlife, including species of endangered birds, salamanders, and fish. Miles of hiking trails wind through a dense native forest, along limestone cliffs, and into areas where water pools in spots perfect for swimming. Walk along the creek for miles, and you'll find plenty of informal, impromptu places to dip in.

Swimming is available all along Barton Creek. Be aware that all swimming at any point along the greenbelt is natural; you swim at your own risk. There are no lifeguards on duty, no structures built around the water, no bathrooms, and no man-made amenities. Be sure to pack in your own drinking water. And, as is true with all natural swim spots, the amount of recent rain in the area will affect water levels.

Multiple access points will get you to the greenbelt. The web address above provides a list of them. Several spots along the creek are well known and are the most popular on hot summer days. Each recommended swim spot is listed under the most conveniently located access point.

AUSTIN AREA

THE FLATS AND CAMPBELL'S HOLE

1601 Spyglass Drive
Austin, TX 78704

ABOUT: Two entrances lead to this tree-lined swim area, where the water rushes over a long series of boulders and crevices known as the Flats before pooling into Campbell's Hole. The entrance on Spyglass Drive is the most direct. It's also conveniently located across the street from a grocery store. Hang a left and you'll come upon the Flats after a half-mile walk (roughly) down a rocky trail that cuts through sycamores, bald cypresses, and leafy brush. Turning right will take you farther down the greenbelt. The other entrance is off Barton Springs Road.

At the Flats the creek's currents are more active than those you'll find at Gus Fruh; this site is popular with a younger crowd, who bring dogs, six-packs, and portable radios to hang out on the flat limestone ledge and in the pockets of water among the many boulders and rocks that jut from the creek bed. Families with small children may prove better served at Gus Fruh. The water at the Flats varies in depth and moves swiftly. You'll find shallow spots to sit in not far from deeper places to submerge. In general, you'll find plenty of nooks and crannies along the banks of the creek to spread out a towel and carve out a little space for yourself. When the rainfall has been good, Campbell's Hole, at the end of the Flats, is a wide, deep swimming hole. A gravel beach on the far side is a good place to dry off.

Parking is on residential streets, and it can be difficult to find a spot. To avoid an endless hunt, consider riding a Capital Metro bus. There's a bus stop directly across the street from the Spyglass entrance.

GUS FRUH

2642 Barton Hills Drive
Austin, TX 78704

ABOUT: You'll find the trailhead to Gus Fruh on Barton Hills Drive, a residential street. There is no parking lot. Find a spot along the curb, and make sure to lock your car and be thoughtful about how you store your valuables. Be mindful of respecting driveways and posted street signs.

The trail at Gus Fruh is part of the Violet Crown Trail, a project that will create a thirty-mile corridor through the greenbelt and into the countryside. It's the work of the Hill Country Conservancy, which seeks to preserve the land and its natural beauty for recreational use.

The trail down to the water splits early on before joining up again. When you're descending to the creek, the trail to the left is

steep and rocky but not difficult. The trail to the right is mostly smooth and rife with switchbacks. Both lead to the water. While both trails can be rocky and uneven in places, neither is difficult to traverse. Either direction guides you through the healthy plant life that gives the greenbelt its name.

The water at Gus Fruh is clear and still, surrounded by syca-more, elm, ash, and juniper trees that offer plenty of shade. The calm water makes this a good spot for families. The shore at Gus Fruh is rocky, as is the creek bed. Swim shoes are recommended to protect toes. This is a very popular spot for people with dogs.

TWIN FALLS AND SCULPTURE FALLS

Barton Creek Greenbelt West (Gaines Creek/Twin Falls)
3918 South MoPac Expressway
Austin, TX 78704

Scottish Woods Trail
Intersection of Scottish Woods Trail and
    Camp Craft Road
Austin, TX 78704

ABOUT: Situated just over a mile apart on a moderate trail, Twin Falls and Sculpture Falls are two of the most idyllic spots for swimming along the Barton Creek Greenbelt. Two access points lead down to the trail: Gaines Creek/Twin Falls access and Scottish Woods Trail.

The Gaines Creek/Twin Falls entry point is a bit unusual as it's right by Loop 360 (aka Capital of Texas Highway), alongside an entrance ramp to MoPac (Loop 1). Parking is available on the side of the road just before the on-ramp. There is no parking lot,

though often cones mark off the area where cars can angle in along the side of the road.

The Gaines Creek/Twin Falls access point will take you along a rocky, uneven trail for just under a half mile before depositing you at Twin Falls, so named because of two short waterfalls that fill a rocky-bottomed pool surrounded by trees, boulders, and limestone. If you continue another mile or so down the trail, you'll reach Sculpture Falls. Keep an eye out for trail markers posted every so often between Twin Falls and Sculpture Falls. They'll let you know you're headed in the right direction and, most important, tell you when to turn off the trail to find Sculpture Falls.

The second access point to Sculpture Falls, the Scottish Woods Trail, starts off with a steep hike up the "Hill of Life." While this access point is a bit easier to get to, and the trail here will take you past several lovely waterfalls, this hill is a challenging start. Wear good walking shoes.

At Sculpture Falls, Barton Creek rushes over enormous boulders to fill another rock-bottomed pool where you can swim or soak in the clear, cold water surrounded by natural limestone and shade trees. Swimming is great both above and below the falls, though take care when the water is high, as the current below can be swift. The swim space here is bigger than at Twin Falls, so if you head into the greenbelt via the Gaines/Twin Falls entry and find Twin Falls full, head on down to Sculpture and try your luck there. Both spots are terrific opportunities to take advantage of the abundant natural environment of the greenbelt and forget that there's a bustling city nearby.

PRO TIP: The biggest threat to Barton Creek, after commercial and residential development in the area, is pollution by its visitors. This is a delicate ecological environment. Be a good steward and do your part to ensure fellow swimmers and nature lovers can enjoy this unique landscape for years to come. Clean up after yourself and your pets. Pack out all trash when you leave.

AUSTIN AREA

Barton Springs Pool

2201 Barton Springs Road
Austin, TX 78704
(512) 867-3080
austintexas.gov/department/barton-springs-pool

HOURS: 5 a.m.–10 p.m. (closed Th 9 a.m.–7 p.m. for cleaning).
ENTRANCE FEES: Resident: $5 adults. $3 ages 12–17. $2 ages
1–11 and 62 and older. Nonresident: $9 adults. $5 ages 12–17. $4
ages 1–11. Free to those under 1. Free to all 5 a.m.–9 a.m. and 9
p.m.–10 p.m. Cash only accepted at the gate. Credit card ticket
kiosks available outside the main gate.

PARK RULES: Coolers, ice chests, thermal bags, food, smoking, glass, alcohol, frisbees, footballs, and hard balls prohibited. Drinks must be in plastic resealable containers with a twist-top lid.

CAMPING: Not available.

ABOUT: Barton Springs Pool is, without a doubt, the most famous natural swim spot in Austin and possibly all of Texas. Located in the center of downtown in beautiful Zilker Park, Barton Springs has long been an urban oasis where Capital City dwellers come to relax, people watch, and cool off in the famously cold waters. The springwater here is a brisk 68° year round.

While three springs (two named for Eliza and Parthenia, daughters of William Barton, who laid claim to the area in the mid-1800s) exist in the area, it is Main Barton Spring, just upstream from the diving board, that feeds the pool swimmers enjoy. The man-made pool enjoyed today was built in the 1920s when two dams were built across Barton Creek to create the current swim area. An extensive walkway and a bathhouse were also built. The bottom of the pool was altered at this time to create a shallow area at one end and eighteen-foot depths at the other. The original 1922 bathhouse was washed away by floods in 1935. The limestone bathhouse that stands today replaced it. Over the years the pool has been the site of everything from baptisms to water pageants to a gathering of thinkers on Philosophers' Rock.

Barton Springs is listed as a federally protected habitat. The water is home to a variety of plant life, fish, and the endangered Barton Springs salamander. In 1990, facing extensive development plans that would harm the springs and their flora and fauna, more than eight hundred people famously filled Austin's city hall for an all-night meeting; the testimonies they delivered blocked the development. The following year more than thirty thousand Austinites signed a petition that established the Save Our Springs Alliance, an organization that continues to educate the public and work to protect the health of the Edwards Aquifer and Barton Springs.

The popularity of Barton Springs cannot be understated. Arrive early to ensure a spot in the parking lot and on the grassy slopes on either side of the water. This is one of the most active recreation areas in a city that is bursting at the seams with residents and tourists. Prepare accordingly. While a large parking lot surrounds the pool, all parking is now metered by the City of Austin.

SWIMMING: The three-acre swimming pool runs as deep as eighteen feet and as long as nine hundred feet, with a lengthy shallow end fit for children and waist-deep wading. All swimming is open; there are no swim lanes. The pool, which features a concrete embankment, metal ladders, and a diving area with a low diving board, was built to maintain some of the area's natural features.

Be brave and jump in; it's the quickest way to let your body acclimate to the shock of the cold water. Lifeguards are on duty 8 a.m.–10 p.m. A trip to Barton Springs is a unique opportunity to feel connected to both the natural and human life of the city. Austin wouldn't be Austin without it.

AMENITIES: Bathhouse. Concession stand. Diving board. Concrete ramp into shallow end.

PRO TIP: If you're looking to add a little magic to your Austin summer evening, go for a night swim at Barton Springs. Admission (and the moonlight) is free from 9 to 10 p.m.

Blanco State Park

101 Park Road 23
Blanco, TX 78606
(830) 833-4333
tpwd.texas.gov/state-parks/blanco

HOURS: 8:15 a.m.–10 p.m.
ENTRANCE FEES: $5 per adult. Free ages 12 and under. Camping fees apply.
PARK RULES: Texas Parks & Wildlife rules apply.
CAMPING: Tent, RV (water and electric hookups), and screened shelters.
ABOUT: Blanco River State Park is a small (for a state park),

105-acre park located in downtown Blanco. Built by the CCC, which also constructed the two stone dams that impound the river, it opened to the public in 1934 and was one of the first four parks built by the CCC in Texas. Just over a half mile of hiking trails give visitors an opportunity to experience a little bit of nature right in the center of town.

The Blanco River begins as a series of springs in Kendall County and flows eastward for eighty-seven miles until it joins the San Marcos River near San Marcos. A shallow river known for its blue-green water, the Blanco is prone to flooding. In 2015 the river rose more than forty feet above its normal level during extreme rainfall, destroying homes and ravaging trees and natural habitats in the process. Damage was severe at Blanco State Park, where park rangers and volunteers worked for months to restore the area and open the park to the public again. Careful use of the river by visitors is vital as the ecological environment continues to recover.

SWIMMING: The river's seven-foot dams make for a unique swimming experience. The dams create platforms that section off the swimming areas. Ladders descend from one platform to the next, allowing swimmers to maneuver between serene and active waters. When the river is up, the dams also create a scenic set of falls. Both sides of the river offer multiple points of access to the water.

AMENITIES: Restrooms. Picnic area with grills. Pavilion. Park store. Canoe and tube rentals. Educational and interpretive programs.

PRO TIP: Make a whole day of this swim excursion and experience the friendly hospitality Blanco has to offer. Real Ale Brewing Company is located here, as well as the Blanco Pioneer Museum and the Uptown Blanco Art Center.

AUSTIN AREA

Blue Hole Park, Georgetown

West 2nd Street and Rock Street
Blue Hole Park Road
Georgetown, TX 78626
parks.georgetown.org/blue-hole

HOURS: Dawn to dusk.

ENTRANCE FEES: Free.

PARK RULES: Glass containers, diving or jumping from cliffs, open fires, prohibited. Pets must be on leash.

CAMPING: Not available.

ABOUT: An hour north of downtown Austin in pretty, tourist-friendly Georgetown is a happening river spot that draws crowds of swimmers to its waters on summer weekends. Blue Hole in Georgetown sits on the South Fork of the San Gabriel River just a few blocks from the town square. A high limestone bluff rises above the river on one side; the other features a wide asphalt walkway and grassy strips for strolling and lounging. There is limited shade here, and space on the grass can fill up during peak months.

SWIMMING: Step right off the rocky bank into the water. Two short, natural waterfalls flow over dips in the riverbed, creating tiered swim areas and plenty of fun for young swimmers who like to frolic in the crashing water. While the space to spread out on the bank is somewhat limited, the river at Blue Hole is wide enough to offer plenty of swim space. The water does get deep, so be sure to fit young swimmers with floaties. No lifeguard is on duty; swim at your own risk. The City of Georgetown does not monitor water flow or bacteria levels.

AMENITIES: Restrooms. Picnic areas. Public parking available on the corner of 3rd Street and Rock Street (lot and garage).

PRO TIP: Take a stroll around downtown Georgetown, a great place to grab lunch or a coffee and do some souvenir shopping.

Blue Hole Regional Park, Wimberley

100 Blue Hole Lane
Wimberley, TX 78676
(512) 660-9111
cityofwimberley.com

HOURS: 9 a.m.–6 p.m. (Memorial Day through Labor Day);
10 a.m.–6 p.m. (weekends only in May).
ENTRANCE FEES: $10 per adult. $6 ages 4–12, military or seniors.
PARK RULES: Alcohol, glass containers, fishing, and smoking prohibited. No grills or pets in the swim area. Ages 12 and under must be accompanied by an adult.
CAMPING: Not available.
ABOUT: Located near the center of scenic, historic Wimberley,

Blue Hole Regional Park is home to one of the most unique and beloved swimming holes in Central Texas. Famous for the old-growth bald cypress trees that ring the pool's depths, this beautiful, coveted spot hits capacity early on a busy summer weekend. When capacity is reached, the swim area is closed for a minimum of two hours.

In 2005, confronted with the possibility of residential development that would sacrifice Blue Hole's natural beauty and compromise its ecosystem, the City of Wimberley launched a successful fundraising campaign to save the park. The passionate efforts of determined community members reserved for public use 126 acres along Cypress Creek. Their work secured the habitats of a variety of native grasses, wildflowers, and wildlife.

SWIMMING: The bald cypress trees surrounding Blue Hole make this an unforgettable swim and offer plenty of shade in between dips. Blue Hole's deep water is accessible via a built-in ladder. After you swim, pull up a length of manicured lawn and dry off while lounging, reading, or picnicking. When the heat creeps up on you again (and you've worked up the nerve), try out the popular rope swing. While the entire park is open year round during regular operating hours, the swimming area is open only during the designated swimming season (typically Memorial Day through Labor Day).

AMENITIES: Clean, modern restrooms with showers. Four miles of trail. Pavilion. Playground. Amphitheater. Picnic area. Basketball and volleyball courts.

PRO TIP: Blue Hole notoriously fills up fast. Have a backup plan in case capacity has been reached by the time you arrive. Either way, make sure to enjoy Wimberley while you're there!

AUSTIN AREA

Bull Creek District Park

6701 Lakewood Drive
Austin, TX 78731
(512) 974-6797
austinparks.org/bull-creek

HOURS: 8 a.m.–10 p.m.

ENTRANCE FEES: Free.

PARK RULES: City of Austin park rules apply.

CAMPING: Not available.

ABOUT: Just off Loop 360 in Austin, near the Pennybacker Bridge, the clear, cool waters of Bull Creek flow down past steep limestone cliffs studded with trees and native plant life to create one of the most rollicking spring-fed swimming holes in the city. Enjoy a bit of live oak shade above a lively, spacious swim area in this accessible stretch of the thirty-two-square-mile Bull Creek watershed.

The Bull Creek Foundation, a nonprofit organization made up of volunteers for the Austin Parks Foundation, maintains Bull Creek District Park, where in addition to a beautiful swimming hole, you'll find basketball and volleyball courts. Given its proximity to the center of Austin and its easy access from Loop 360, this is a highly popular spot in the hot summer months. While the park is part of the Austin Parks Foundation, the swimming hole is undeveloped and unsupervised. Amenities are not available. Bring plenty of water.

SWIMMING: Bull Creek streams down over rock faces that create a natural waterslide busy with delighted young swimmers all summer long. From the foot of that slide, the creek widens into a long, spacious swimming hole surveyed by an Edwards limestone cliff face shaded by oaks, pecans, and junipers. Wide shelves of limestone around the swim area provide plenty of space to set up in a sunny spot. Water level depends on rainfall.

No lifeguard is on duty; swim at your own risk. This is a beautiful spot to escape city life and appreciate the natural terrain of Travis County.

AMENITIES: Parking is available just above the swim area, and overflow parking is just across the street.

PRO TIP: Don't be shy. Join the kids and ride the falls—at least once.

Canyon Lake Park

US Army Corps of Engineers
Canyon Lake Office
601 C.O.E. Road
Canyon Lake, TX 78133

HOURS: (Canyon Beach Park) M–F 1 p.m. to dusk; Sa–Su and holidays, 8 a.m. to dusk. Open summers only.

ENTRANCE FEES: $5 per vehicle (maximum eight people ages 13 and older per vehicle). $2 for each additional person ages 13 and older. $2 per walk-in ages 13 and older.

PARK RULES: Pets, glass containers, camping on beaches, and firearms prohibited.

CAMPING: Tent and RV camping at specific parks around the lake.

ABOUT: On the edge of the Balcones escarpment, Canyon Lake Dam impounds the Guadalupe River to form Canyon Lake, which was completed in 1964 for the purpose of flood control and conservation of the Guadalupe River basin. The parks on the lake are maintained and operated by the Army Corps of Engineers.

SWIMMING: While visitors may swim as they choose anywhere along the shoreline of Canyon Lake, there are two designated swim beaches open to the public. A third designated beach at Potters Creek Park is open to campers only. Canyon Beach Park, located on the north shore of the lake near Hancock, offers a long, unshaded grass shore that opens directly into the warm lake water. The bottom of the lake is pebbled, with soft spots here and there. The swim area is roped off and relatively shallow, reaching between five and six feet by the buoy border. This is a popular spot for families, as the shallow water offers a good opportunity for young swimmers to splash around and is an easy spot for anyone to float. Comal Park, located on the south shore of the lake near Startzville, offers a day-use swim area with a sandy beach and a long, narrow swim area marked by buoys. Loaner life jackets are available at Comal Park beach. The wake of motorized watercraft affects both beaches.

AMENITIES: Restrooms.

PRO TIP: Located off the busy I-35 corridor just north of New Braunfels, Canyon Lake is an easy day trip for residents and tourists of San Antonio and Austin who want to get away from it all without trekking too far from home base.

Colorado Bend State Park

Off FM 580, 10 miles south of Bend on "Dirt Road"
Bend, TX 76824
(325) 628-3240
tpwd.texas.gov/state-parks/colorado-bend

HOURS: 6 a.m.–10 p.m.

ENTRANCE FEES: $5 per adult. Free ages 12 and under. Camping fees apply.

PARK RULES: Texas Parks & Wildlife rules apply.

CAMPING: Tent, RV (water and electric hookups), screened shelters, and cabins.

ABOUT: With thirty-two miles of hiking trails, 5,300 acres of natural landscape, more than four hundred underground caves, an abundance of campsites, and one of the prettiest series of swimming holes in the state, Colorado Bend State Park is a highly popular place for Central Texans to enjoy the outdoors. Six miles of the Colorado River flow through this park, which is situated north of Buchanan Lake and just west of Lampasas. The best swimming, however, is all thanks to Spicewood Springs.

SWIMMING: A grassy, half-mile walk from the parking lot down Spicewood Springs Trail takes you to the bottom of a series of swimming holes fed by Spicewood Springs. You'll find a flat shelf of rock that's an easy spot for swimmers to refresh in the water that flows from above. Cross this slippery rock and hike up to discover additional swimming holes, some small and shallow, some deeper and longer. Springwater cascades from one hole to the next until it hits that final, wide granite shelf where people wade and kids slide.

The bottoms of the swim holes vary from soft in some places to rocky in others. The granite shelf at the bottom of the trail is quite slick. Water shoes are highly recommended. This is an undeveloped, totally natural area. The trail to the upper swim-ming holes is dirt and rock. Access to the upper swim spots can be a bit treacherous and requires careful steps and sure footing over narrow, wet rock. Leave your beach gear behind, as there really isn't a good place to post up a butterfly chair or park a cooler. Bring a towel, water shoes, sun block, bottled water, and your balance.

The swim areas are not big enough for long-range swimming. These are spots to sit, soak, and hang out surrounded by lush vegetation.

AMENITIES: Modern restrooms with showers. Picnic areas. Park store. Playground.

PRO TIP: Don't miss the opportunity to check out Gorman Falls or go on a guided cave tour.

Deep Eddy Pool

> 401 Deep Eddy Drive
> Austin, 78703
> (512) 974-1189
> austintexas.gov/department/deep-eddy-pool

HOURS: 8 a.m.–8 p.m. (May–Oct.); lap swimming only M–F 8 a.m.–10 a.m.

ENTRANCE FEES: Residents: $5 adult. $3 ages 12–17. $2 ages 1–11. $2 ages 62 and older. Free for children under 1. Nonresidents: $9 adult. $5 ages 12–17. $4 ages 1–11. $5 ages 62 and older. Free for children under 1. Cash and credit cards accepted.

PARK RULES: Alcohol, tobacco products and e-cigarettes, glass, and profanity prohibited. Food, coolers, and sugary beverages prohibited in the swim area. Proper swimwear must be worn in the water; no cutoffs or street clothing.

CAMPING: Not available.

ABOUT: A haven for Austinites in the long summer months, spring-fed Deep Eddy Pool is notable as the first outdoor concrete swimming pool in the state of Texas. Smaller than Barton Springs, Deep Eddy is tucked away on Lake Austin Boulevard in a spot that tends to escape the sight of tourists. This is a place where families bring itty-bitty swimmers to test the cold water in the shallow end, friends unpack the events of the day in the shade, and lap swimmers take advantage of the several dedicated swim lanes.

Deep Eddy was once a natural swimming hole surrounded by a limestone ledge. In 1902 the property owner established Deep Eddy Resort, the first park and recreation area in Austin. The resort sold the land to A. J. Eilers in 1915, who teamed up with a former circus promoter to create a veritable aquatic theater, featuring attractions such as a trapeze, Ferris wheel, and Great Lorena's Diving Horse. Check out more fun historical facts with a look at the Deep Eddy Mural Project, a mosaic wall at the east end of the park. Today, three wells pump natural springwater into a pool that, while no longer open to diving horses, continues to draw swimmers looking to refresh themselves in the midst of city living.

SWIMMING: Most attractive about Deep Eddy, in addition to its clear, clean water, is the neat way the pool divides its varying depths. The shallow end with its sloping entrance is roped off from an area three to four feet deep where floaters lounge; that area is separated from the swim lanes by a wall. The swim lanes are roped off from a nearly eight-foot-deep diving section on the far side of the pool. Metal ladders offer easy access into the cold water. Lifeguards are on duty.

A concrete path encompasses the pool; grassy lawns slope on all but the south side of the water. Families with small children tend to congregate on the west end near the shallow water, while adult swimmers tend to spread their blankets on the flat grass near the deep end.

AMENITIES: Bathhouse. Concession stand. Pool lift for handicap access.

PRO TIP: If the small parking lot is full, find parking on Veterans Drive. After your swim, make a beeline for Magnolia Cafe on the other side of Lake Austin Boulevard or hit up JuiceLand right around the corner.

Emma Long Metropolitan Park

1600 City Park Road
Austin, TX 78730
(512) 974-1831
austintexas.gov/department
   /emma-long-metropolitan-park

HOURS: 7 a.m.–10 p.m.

ENTRANCE FEES: M-Th $5 per car; F–Su and holidays $10 per car. Credit cards only, no cash. Camping fees apply.

PARK RULES: Styrofoam, smoking, and glass containers prohibited. No collecting firewood. Pets must be on leash.

CAMPING: Tent and RV (water and electric hookups) reservations available.

ABOUT: Half an hour northwest of downtown Austin, Emma Long Metropolitan Park is a 1,147-acre park on the Lake Austin impoundment of the Colorado River. Popular with families and folks looking to cut loose and set up camp for the afternoon or overnight, Emma Long is a great place to grill, play music, socialize, splash, and soak. You'll find plenty of kids racing around with floating noodles and inflatable tubes enjoying over a mile of lakefront and easy access to the water.

The park is named for city councilwoman Emma Long, a veritable force of nature in Austin politics and the first woman to serve on the city council. Elected in 1948, Long established herself as a representative of the people, fighting for workers' rights, fair housing and desegregation, and equal rights for all Austinites regardless of economic status or skin color. She revived the Parks and Recreation Board, worked to clean up the city's streets, and ran a famous poker game at her house for decades. She was Austin's first female mayor pro tem and was named an advisor to the United Nations, among many other achievements. The park was named after her in 1984.

SWIMMING: While the water is easily accessible all along the bank, there is a roped-off, shallow swim area with a strip of sandy beach good for young swimmers. The lake bottom is soft and sandy. While a no-wake zone is in place, the lake is narrow enough here that the frequent motor boats and Jet Skis keep the water lapping at the bank and the knees of the cypress trees that grow along the water's edge. No lifeguard is on duty; swim at your own risk.

AMENITIES: Restroom with showers. Picnic area with grills. Sand volleyball court. Basketball hoops. Hiking trails. Boat ramp.

PRO TIP: Resources at Emma Long can be overwhelmed on busy summer weekends. Grab an early swim before heading out for a day in Austin or exploring more of the area's parks.

Hamilton Pool Preserve

24300 Hamilton Pool Rd.
Dripping Springs, TX 78620
(512) 264-2740
parks.traviscountytx.gov/parks/hamilton-pool-preserve

HOURS: 9 a.m.–1 p.m., 2 p.m.–6 p.m., weather permitting. Reservations do not guarantee swimming and are required Mar.1–Oct. 31, Nov–Feb on Sa–Su, and on Travis County holidays. Swimming ends 30 minutes prior to the end of the reservation period.
ENTRANCE FEES: $11 advance reservation fee must be paid online, credit cards only. Additional $15 on-site admission must

be paid upon arrival, cash only. Reservations not refundable. Reservations do not guarantee swimming and are required March 1–Oct. 31, Sa, Su, and on Travis County holidays. Call the park to confirm swim conditions. For full reservation details, visit parks.traviscountytx.gov/reservations/hamilton-pool Nov–Feb.

PARK RULES: Pets, glass, and public display of alcohol consumption prohibited. Visitors must remain on trails.

CAMPING: Not available.

ABOUT: Thousands of years of erosion have formed a remarkable otherworldly spot in the center of Texas where water from Hamilton Creek plummets fifty feet into a serene jade pool beneath a collapsed grotto. Even more fantastic? This spot is a short drive from Austin—and swimming is welcome.

The first thing to know about Hamilton Pool, aside from its surreal beauty, is that it's extremely popular and reservations, which are required, are booked weeks in advance. The second thing to know is that it's a nature preserve first and a swimming hole second. When Travis County acquired the 232 acres that include the grotto from the Reimers family in 1985, decades of livestock grazing and unrestricted public use had severely damaged the natural ecosystems. The county has put significant work into rehabilitating the delicate environment. Preservation is an ongoing process that benefits from our participation and cooperation.

When you do make it into Hamilton, you'll understand the draw. The limestone outcroppings, stalactites, abundant moss, and plummeting fifty-foot waterfall are unforgettable. Hike the nature trail (one of the most overlooked hikes in Travis County, according to one park ranger) and keep an eye out for seashell fossils. During the Cretaceous period, much of Central Texas was underwater. Look closely and you'll discover the ancient imprints of marine life in the rocks. The boulders in the water itself are a good place to spot these pieces of history as well.

From the parking area there is a steep quarter-mile walk

AUSTIN AREA

on uneven terrain down to the water. Sure footwear is recommended. There is no potable water available, so bring your own drinking water.

SWIMMING: A short pebbled shore lines the water as you enter the grotto. Visitors often lay out towels and set up chairs here, treating the low hill as a beach. Walk into the bright water and swim out to the waterfall or simply bask in the view of the overhang. A path to the left takes you beneath the overhang, through narrow crevices between rocks, and around to the area behind the waterfall. From here, swimmers often jump into the water from the low rocks. There's truly nothing like this swim experience at any other public spot in Texas.

AMENITIES: Restrooms. Hiking trails. Picnic tables.

PRO TIP: If you do not have a reservation, do not show up at Hamilton Pool. The pool is typically booked at least two weeks in advance. Do your part to preserve this rare spot: stay on the trails, pick up after yourself, and obey all posted signs and instructions from park rangers.

Hippie Hollow/ McGregor County Park

7000 Comanche Trail
Austin, TX 78732
parks.traviscountytx.gov/parks/hippie-hollow

HOURS: 9 a.m. to dusk.

ENTRANCE FEES: $15 per car. $8 per pedestrian or cyclist. Cash only. Must be at least 18 to enter.

PARK RULES: Clothing optional. Nudity is not permitted in the

parking lot. Pets, glass, public display and consumption of alcohol, and open fireworks prohibited. Grills are permitted.

CAMPING: Not available.

ABOUT: Originally known as McGregor County Park, Hippie Hollow, located in the Hill Country about thirty minutes west of Austin on the north shore of Lake Travis, is the only clothing-optional park in Texas. It came by its name and nature in the 1970s, when skinny-dipping became the norm and authorities gave up prosecuting it. Owned by the LCRA and leased to Travis County Parks since 1985, this 109-acre park caters to adults who enjoy the ultimate free-swim experience. While nudity is welcome, lewd behavior is not permitted and respect for everyone's privacy is expected. Some areas of the park are a preserved habitat protected by the Federal Endangered Species Act and are off-limits to visitors.

SWIMMING: The shoreline along Lake Travis at Hippie Hollow runs for approximately one-third of a mile and features large rocks that step down toward the water. The slope can be quite steep in some places. A concrete path runs above the bank, offering access down to the water via sets of steps and trails along the way. Head left down the concrete path when you enter and eventually you'll come upon a small cove roped off from the rest of the lake. Here, the slope down to the water is not so steep, though close-toed shoes are recommended for traversing the terrain. While the uneven, rocky shore provides plenty of jutting rocks to set up a spot, you may want more than a towel to sit on if you're going to be there all day. Access to the water is natural; expect to climb in and out over rocks at water level. No lifeguard is on duty; swim at your own risk.

AMENITIES: Restrooms. Picnic areas. Potable water. Nature and hiking trails.

PRO TIP: If you're going to get into the spirit, make sure you put sunblock where the sun don't typically shine.

Jacob's Well Natural Area

1699 Mount Sharp Road
Wimberley, TX 78676
(512) 214-4593
hayscountytx.com/departments/hays-county-parks
-recreation/jacobs-well-natural-area

HOURS: 8 a.m.–6 p.m. (May 1 to Sept. 30).

ENTRANCE FEES: $9 per adult. $5 ages 5–12, seniors 60 and older, and veterans. Free ages 4 and under. $5 per Hayes County resident. Reservations are required and may only be made online at jwna.checkfront.com/reserve.

Payment is at the gate upon arrival. Credit and debit cards only, no cash. Capacity is limited to three hundred swimmers per day, in groups of sixty. Swim sessions are limited to two hours. No fee is required to park and enter the nature preserve.

PARK RULES: Scuba diving, diving from rocks, pets, smoking, firearms, glass containers, and alcohol prohibited. Do not remove any natural items or artifacts from the grounds.

CAMPING: Not available.

ABOUT: One of the most well-known swimming spots in Central Texas is Jacob's Well, located in the Hill Country a short drive from downtown Wimberley. Ethereal blue-green water covers the mouth of a mile-long series of limestone tunnels and caves, one of the longest such underwater systems in Texas. Jacob's Well is named after Jacob de Cordova, Wimberley's first land promoter. Preserved by Hayes County with the help of the Nature Conservancy of Texas and Wimberley Valley Watershed Association, Jacob's Well is an artesian spring and the source of Cypress Creek and Blue Hole. Once upon a time, the artesian spring gushed six feet or more in the air. Over time, however, as development has increased and thousands of wells now draw from the Trinity Aquifer, the spring's phenomenal pressure has

diminished. What remains is a calm swim spot above the deep, dark mystery of the caves.

SWIMMING: Capacity is often reached on the weekends, so be sure to make reservations early and prepare to share the swim space. Swimmers must maneuver down a short, steep trail from the cliff top to the water. Swim shoes are recommended, as surfaces can be quite slippery. Enjoy swimming above the mouth of the well, where the springwater is a cool 68° year round, and along the long, shallow swim shelf that extends beyond it. The series of tunnels and underwater chambers are off limits; a single errant kick can stir up the fine silt on a chamber floor and cloud vision and judgment. Above the water a rich riparian area is home to a wide variety of vegetation and wildlife. No lifeguard is on duty; swim at your own risk.

AMENITIES: No facilities available.

PRO TIP: Novel to toss in your bag for the trip: *Jacob's Well*, by Texas author Stephen Harrigan.

Krause Springs

404 Krause Springs Road
Spicewood, TX 78669
(830) 693-4181
krausesprings.net

HOURS: 9 a.m.–9 p.m. (peak season); 9 a.m.–8 p.m. otherwise. Open year round, though occasionally closed Dec.– Feb. for property improvements. Krause Springs will not close due to drought or flooding.

ENTRANCE FEES: $8 per adult. $5 ages 4–11. Free ages 4 and under. Camping fees apply. Cash only. Pay at the main house upon arrival (where you'll also find one of Krause's most charming features, a peaceful butterfly garden with benches, flower gardens, and large wind chimes).

PARK RULES: Pets, smoking, glass containers, jumping from bluff, and open carry of firearms prohibited.

CAMPING: Primitive, tent, and RV (water and electric hookups). Reservations required for RV camping. No reservations required for tent sites.

ABOUT: Privately owned and maintained by the Krause family, Krause Springs is a well-tended and thoughtfully landscaped 115-acre spot beloved by locals for its easy swimming and camping experiences. Elton and Jane Krause purchased the land in 1955 and built the spring-fed swimming pool on site, as well as the gazebo, fountain, stone picnic benches, and many other conveniences. Thirty-two springs water the property. As you explore the grounds, keep an eye out for waterfalls. Krause Springs is listed on the National Register of Historic Places as an undisturbed Native American burial ground.

SWIMMING: Krause has two spots for swimming. You'll find a seventy-by-twenty-foot spring-fed, man-made pool as you make your way toward the path that takes you down to the natural swimming hole. This pool is a good spot for young or inexperienced swimmers to enjoy the water without concern over sudden changes in depth. Stone benches and a concrete embankment surround the pool.

From the pool head down a set of limestone steps to reach the natural swimming hole. Shaded by bald cypress trees and rimmed with mossy banks and wide limestone rocks that create a serene swimming cove, this oasis has been lovingly preserved in its natural state. The unshaded limestone bank is a perfect place to sprawl out and sunbathe. Continue along the bank to an area where bald cypresses offer shady spots to post up for the day. Access to the water is natural here. Expect to maneuver in and out of the water off the lips of rocks and the knees of cypress trees. Also expect to meet many other swimmers during the summer months; Krause is one of the most frequented swimming holes in the area.

Swim shoes are recommended, as the rock does get quite slippery. Diving is not permitted. A rope swing hangs on the far side of the hole. Tubes are welcome, though not available to rent. Small kayaks are welcome, but be aware that entering the water at the natural pool may be difficult during the crowded summer months at this highly popular spot. No lifeguard is on duty; swim at your own risk.

AMENITIES: Bathrooms with sinks, stalls, and spring-fed showers. Barbecue pits (personal pits welcome, provided they do not sit on the ground). Snack concession during the summer. Firewood available for purchase in the main office.

PRO TIP: Sit a spell in the butterfly garden when you arrive and enjoy the tones of the Texas-sized wind chimes.

Landa Park

164 Landa Park Drive
New Braunfels, TX 78130
(830) 221-4360
nbtexas.org/156/Landa-Park

HOURS: Landa Park Aquatic Complex hours vary by season. Call ahead or visit the website to determine when the complex is open for swimming.

ENTRANCE FEES: M–F $6 per adult, $5 seniors age 60 or more and children ages 3–12, $2 per spectator. Sa–Su $8 per adult, $7 seniors age 60 or more and children ages 3–12, $4 per spectator. Children ages 3 and under free.

PARK RULES: Glass, Styrofoam, alcohol, smoking or tobacco use, pop-up tents, grills, and non-USCG approved floatation devices prohibited in Aquatic Complex. Children ages 11 and under must be accompanied by an adult.

CAMPING: Not available.

ABOUT: Landa Park is a large, bustling park along the Comal River in New Braunfels that offers a variety of activities for visitors. Popular with family picnickers who plant pop-up tents and grill the weekend days away, Landa offers miniature golf, paddleboats, a train ride for kids, and more attractions set among ancient oak trees. While there is a significant amount of riverfront here, Landa is in an environmentally sensitive area and access to the water is restricted. Nowhere else in Texas will you find so many artesian springs—more than a dozen— bubbling up in one place. The springs feed the two-and-a-half-mile-long Comal River, whose headwaters are at Comal Springs inside the park.

SWIMMING: Swimming is permitted in two specifically designated areas. A hotel and bathhouse built by German settlers in the early 1900s remain part of the Landa Park Aquatics Complex, which offers a spring-fed pool on one side and an Olympic-sized swimming pool on the other. The spring-fed pool has been outfitted with several slides, a zip line, and a splash pad. Lifeguards are on duty. This child-friendly area is crowded during peak seasons.

For free swimming at Landa Park, head to the wading pool. This shallow spot offers easy floating for kids with small tubes and floatation devices. A ramp provides access to the water. While also crowded, the limited space in the wading area and its shallow depth make for a more contained swim experience. This spot is good for particularly young or new swimmers.

AMENITIES: Restrooms. Picnic areas with grills. Drinking fountains. Sand volleyball courts. Horseshoe pits. Playscapes.

PRO TIP: Visit Founders' Oak, one of the park's ancient oak trees. A plaque at the base of the tree notes it was planted as a seedling in 1700, when the area was a campsite for Native Americans who used the oak's limbs, according to legend, to indicate direction to future fellow travelers.

Laura Reed Park

West Reed Park Road
Jonestown, TX 78645

HOURS: Open 24/7.

ENTRANCE FEES: Free.

PARK RULES: Glass containers and fireworks prohibited.

CAMPING: Not available.

ABOUT: Laura Reed Park is a small, primitive park along Lake Travis, bisected by West Reed Road (off FM 1431, south of Jonestown). There are no signs indicating you've found it. Look for a flat gravel space on the side of the road and a sign that prohibits boat trailer parking. Park there and head for the trail down to the water. This spot is better suited for adventurous adult swimmers. The trail is unkempt, uneven, rocky, and quite steep. Erosion around tracks from vehicular traffic (now prohibited) has created deep ruts that can make this a challenge to navigate. Reliable shoes are highly recommended.

SWIMMING: At the bottom of the trail, look right to find a narrow path down to the small, sloping beach. You'll find approximately thirty yards of rocky lakeshore facing the back of a boat dock. Because of the dock, the swim spot is protected and secluded. You won't be swimming out into the larger lake here; this is a wild, undesignated pocket of water that will feel like your own secret swim spot.

AMENITIES: None available.

PRO TIP: When you've had your fill of Laura Reed, check out Dave Reed Park, which is also nearby.

Mansfield Dam Park

4370 Mansfield Dam Park Road
Austin, TX 78732
parks.traviscountytx.gov/parks/mansfield-dam

HOURS: Sunrise to sunset.

ENTRANCE FEES: $10 per vehicle. $3 per pedestrian or cyclist. Free for seniors 62 and older and Lone Star veterans. Cash or check only; credit and debit cards not accepted.

PARK RULES: Glass containers, Styrofoam, and smoking prohibited. Pets must be on leash.

CAMPING: Not available.

ABOUT: Mansfield Dam Park is a great, family-friendly destination with several recreational amenities, including a nice picnic area right by the water, a small rock-climbing wall, chess tables, and a life jacket loaner station. For all of the traffic and activity here, the park is clean, manicured, and well maintained. Take a stroll down the hike and bike trail between swims or simply enjoy the fine view from your spot along the water. Mansfield Dam, a joint project of Travis County and the LCRA, was completed in 1941 and forms Lake Travis, the largest Colorado River reservoir and the next to last of the Highland Lakes.

SWIMMING: The primary swim spot at this park is the swim cove at the end of the parking lot. Here a set of picnic tables beneath a crop of cypress trees offers a place to picnic, drape a towel, and get into the water. A wheelchair-accessible concrete walkway with a railing leads down to the lakeshore. There is a shallow, roped-off swim area, though visitors swim just about anywhere in the park they can reach the water. A jetty extends into the lake, providing an easy place to jump in. As you head through the parking lot on your way to the swim cove, on your left you'll find a ladder and concrete steps down to the lake. Just maintain fifty feet between yourself and the boat ramp at all times, in any direction. No lifeguard is on duty; swim at your own risk.

AMENITIES: Restrooms. Picnic areas with grills. Playscape. Boat ramp.

PRO TIP: For a more private experience, snag one of the picnic spots near the stairs that access the water on the left-hand side of the parking lot. On your way out, check out the dam overlook across the street from the park entrance.

McKinney Falls State Park

5808 McKinney Falls Parkway
Austin, TX 78744
(512) 243-1643
tpwd.texas.gov/parks/mckinney-falls

HOURS: 7 a.m.–10 p.m.

ENTRANCE FEES: $6 per adult. Free ages 12 and under. Camping fees apply.

PARK RULES: Texas Parks & Wildlife rules apply.

CAMPING: Tent, RV (water and electric hookups), screened shelters, and cabins.

ABOUT: Located just thirteen miles from the center of Austin, McKinney Falls State Park offers 725 acres of land for camping, hiking, exploring, and swimming in Onion Creek. It also offers an interesting piece of geologic history. An otherwise unassuming hill—now known as Pilot Knob—to the southeast of the park is the remains of what was an active volcano roughly eighty million years ago. During the Cretaceous period, when the center of the state was underwater and dinosaurs roamed Texas, volcanic explosions shaped the land. Lingering volcanic material is still visible beneath the limestone overhangs at the Upper and Lower Falls.

Today, McKinney Falls State Park is one of the most popular spots in the Austin area for outdoor recreation and swimming. It's also home to one of the state's oldest public bald cypress trees, "Old Baldy," estimated to be five hundred years old.

SWIMMING: There are two good swim sites at McKinney Falls: the Upper and Lower Falls. The Upper Falls are a very short walk from the parking lot. Here Onion Creek crashes over limestone to create a pool of water lined with a gravel beach and cypress trees down below. A wide stretch of limestone above the falls creates ample space for sitting and sunning. The Upper

Falls are particularly good for swimming after a good rain (though be aware that a heavy rain will flood the creek). The water here is typically deeper than what you'll find at Lower Falls and makes this the more popular destination.

Head to Lower Falls and you'll find Onion Creek plunging eight feet over a limestone shelf to create yet another swim spot lined with a gravel beach. You'll cross a significant expanse of limestone before arriving at the falls and gravel beach.

AMENITIES: Restrooms. More than eight miles of hiking trails. Picnic areas. Park store.

PRO TIP: Don't be alarmed if a summer day hike through the park deposits you in the middle of a troupe of kids and adults engaged in lively cosplay. That's just Camp Half-Blood.

Milton Reimers Ranch Park

23610 Hamilton Rd.
Dripping Springs, TX 78620
(512) 854-7275
parks.traviscountytx.gov/parks/reimers-ranch

HOURS: 7:00 a.m. to dusk.

ENTRANCE FEES: $10 per vehicle. Cash or check only. Free for seniors ages 62 and older and for disabled veterans.

PARK RULES: Travis County Park rules apply. Pets must remain on leash. Glass bottles and public display of alcohol consumption prohibited. Grills are permitted, but must be above ground.

CAMPING: Not available.

ABOUT: Milton Reimers Ranch marks the largest land acquisition in the history of Travis County and the largest park in its purview. Located just down the road from Hamilton Pool, this massive 2,427-acre Travis County park is an impressive example of the quintessential beauty of the Central Texas landscape. Limestone escarpments, cedar, and scrub brush surround more than three miles of continuous frontage along the Pedernales River. Enjoy a scenic drive into the park along a winding road that offers unobstructed views of the natural environment. The park also provides ample opportunities for rock climbing, mountain biking, and hiking on more than eighteen miles of trails. An easy forty-five-minute drive out of Austin, this is a popular spot to soak up some peace and quiet.

SWIMMING: Multiple marked trails off from the main road provide access to the river, though the trails further into the park require climbing in order to reach the water. The easiest and most pleasant river access for swimmers is available via River Trail, the second trail you'll find on your left as you drive into the park. This stretch of the Pedernales at Reimers Ranch is typically calmer than what you'll find at Pedernales Falls

State Park. Be advised that wherever you access the water at Reimers Ranch, the opposite bank is private property.

From the parking lot, River Trail is a relatively short, occasionally steep concrete path that leads to a plateau where swimmers have two routes to the water: a wheelchair-accessible paved trail to the left and a primitive trail to the right. The primary swim spot is to the left, where the paved trail leads to a curving, rocky beach that faces a picturesque escarpment. Be aware that the signs indicating "Beach Access" are set further in from the turnoff, close to the portable toilets. The riverfront beach here slopes right into the clear, cool, spring-fed Pedernales, providing easy walk-in access to the water. The river bottom is mostly firm and pebbled with stones of varying sizes. If you're going to post up for the day, be sure to bring your own shade and to come prepared either with chairs or enough padding to comfortably sit on the rocks.

The primitive trail to the right (marked with a "River Access" sign) is rocky and uneven, and requires careful footwork to reach a grassy, undeveloped bank with vegetation. Access to the water is less direct than it is at the beach and requires maneuvering over the uneven bank. The bottom of the river is muddier here. This spot does offer soft, grassy space to spread out a blanket and is a bit more secluded than the swim beach.

AMENITIES: Clean restrooms available in the parking lot at River Trail trailhead; portable toilets available closer to the swim beach. More than eighteen miles of hiking, biking, and equestrian trails. Rock climbing.

PRO TIP: The drive between Pedernales Falls State Park and Milton Reimers Ranch is short and scenic. If you have time, it's worth visiting both in a day. Also consider scheduling a guided tour of Pogue Springs Preserve, an undisturbed natural wonderland of spring-fed pools, caves, and escarpments.

Muleshoe Bend Recreation Area

2820 County Road 414
Spicewood, TX 78669
(512) 473-3366
lcra.org/parks/pages/muleshoe-bend.aspx

HOURS: Dawn to dusk.

ENTRANCE FEES: $5 per adult. $2 for disabled and seniors 65 and older. Free ages 12 and under. Camping fees apply.

PARK RULES: Glass containers, public consumption or display of alcoholic beverages, open fires, and firearms prohibited. Intoxicated persons are not permitted on LCRA land. Pets must be on leash.

CAMPING: Tent sites with water views.

ABOUT: Northwest of Austin, on a bend of Lake Travis, sits Muleshoe Bend Recreation Area, a sprawling 920-acre park that boasts six miles of waterfront, six and a half miles of mountain bike trails, horseback riding, camping, and one of the prettiest, most beloved Texas sights to behold in the spring: acres of bluebonnets. This is an easy place to claim some personal space and enjoy big views of the water and the flowers.

SWIMMING: Access to the water is easy along the shallow shoreline. There's plenty of grassy bank to spread out for the day. Depending on the time of year and the water level, you'll find anywhere from a dozen to hundreds of acres of bluebonnets along the riverbank at Muleshoe. This is a well-known spot to see and pose for pictures with the state flower.

AMENITIES: Latrines throughout park. Potable water and restrooms by the main entrance. Picnic areas. No other potable water is available; bring your own. Horseback riding.

PRO TIP: Visit in spring to see acres of bluebonnets in all their glory.

Pace Bend Park

2805 Pace Bend Park Road North
Spicewood, TX 78669
(512) 264-1482
parks.traviscountytx.gov/parks/pace-bend

HOURS: Dawn to dusk.

ENTRANCE FEES: $10 per car. $3 per pedestrian or cyclist. Free for seniors 62 and older and veterans. Cash or check only. Camping fees apply.

PARK RULES: Styrofoam, glass containers, smoking, and gathering firewood prohibited. Pets must be on leash.

CAMPING: Primitive, tent, and RV (water and electric hookups).

ABOUT: A popular spot on Lake Travis, Pace Bend Park is an easy drive west out of Austin to the edge of the Texas Hill Country. Here you'll find nine miles of shoreline, limestone cliffs, miles of hiking trails, and plenty of places to get into the water in a largely undeveloped natural environment.

Pace Bend Road runs in a seven-mile paved loop around the peninsula, with offshoots to various trails and swim spots as it curves around. Signage is simple and unobtrusive on the main road. Roads branching off from Pace Bend Road are also paved and marked with simple signs that don't offer directionals or information beyond labels. Be sure to pick up a map at the entrance booth (or print one from the Texas Parks & Wildlife website) and keep it handy. The eastern and northern sides of the park have shorelines that slope down into the lake. The western side is all high limestone cliffs, coves, and beautiful views.

SWIMMING: There are three designated swim areas in Pace Bend Park: Mudd Cove, Kate's Cove, and Gracy's Cove. All three spots are clearly designated on the park map.

Mudd Cove, on the northeastern side of the park, offers a straightforward swim experience. Cypress trees shade a scattering of picnic benches and campsites that sit close to the water. While day use is welcome here, you will be quite close to these campsites. The lake is easily accessible. You can walk right in from the grassy, sandy bank, which curves around and faces houses and residential property on the opposite shore.

Kate's Cove, the northernmost point of the park and located between two private camps, can feel a bit more spacious and secluded than Mudd Cove; there are considerably more cypress trees marking off campsites and offering both shade and a measure of privacy for campers and day users. The curving, sandy shore presents easy, walk-in access to the water, where you'll find a pebbled lake bottom dotted with plant life. This is a peaceful spot with a prettier view than Mudd Cove.

AUSTIN AREA

Of the three designated swim spots in Pace Bend Park, Gracy's Cove is the most impressive. This roped-off inlet of deep water flows between high, tree-topped limestone cliffs. Set off and protected from the speedboats and their wake, this is a serene spot solely for swimmers, great for floating and basking in the beauty of the lake. Park at the end of the road and prepare to descend a short rocky trail from a small camping area to the limestone cliff where you can pick a spot to set down a towel or chair. The cliff is unshaded here. Access the water by lowering yourself from the rocks (and take note of where you can most easily pull yourself back up onto the rock ledge when you're done swimming). The cove is narrow enough to float or swim to the other side, where some shade is available.

Finding the right access point to Gracy's Cove can be tricky, as several roads marked either N. Gracy or S. Gracy turn off from Pace Bend Road. Look for N. Thurman/S. Gracy Road. From the pay station, take a left then keep to the right. The roads into Gracy's Cove are paved but narrow. Take it slow and be prepared to pull to the side as best you can to let any oncoming traffic pass. The tricky turn and narrow road are worth it; you will be rewarded with a beautiful, hard-to-leave scene.

AMENITIES: Latrines available at each swim area. Picnic areas with grills. Potable water.

PRO TIP: Bring all the supplies you'll need for a day or overnight, as there are limited resources in the immediate surrounding area. If you're planning to camp, beat the crowds and book a campsite in advance.

The Point at Bob Wentz Park

7144 Comanche Trail
Austin TX 78732
parks.traviscountytx.gov/parks/bob-wentz

HOURS: 8 a.m. to dusk.

ENTRANCE FEES: $10 per vehicle. $3 for pedestrians and cyclists. Free for veterans and seniors ages 62 and older. Cash or check only.

PARK RULES: Glass containers, fireworks, and ground fires prohibited. Public display and consumption of alcohol prohibited.

CAMPING: Not available.

ABOUT: Bob Wentz Park is a Travis County Park just a short drive down Comanche Trail from Hippie Hollow on the north shore of Lake Travis. This spot is about half an hour from Austin, making it popular with Capital City residents looking to grab an easy day on the water. The Point at Bob Wentz, a sandy peninsula with significant water access, is packed during the summer weekends. Hang a right as you enter on Bob Wentz Park Road to head toward the Point. The road crosses an inlet and ends at two parking areas on either side. A short walk from the lots takes you to a circular grassy area with picnic tables shaded by colorful canvas awnings. This park often does reach capacity. When the lots are full, vehicles are allowed in on a five out/five in basis.

SWIMMING: The water can be accessed from anywhere around the peninsula, though some spots will have you climbing over boulders. The best access is from a designated swim beach where you can walk right into the water. The shores and lake bottom here are quite rocky. It's important to note that in addition to smaller rocks and pebbles, larger flat stones line the bottom in spots not far from shore, creating unpredictable drop-offs. Life jackets are highly recommended for young swimmers and are available at a life jacket loaner station near the restrooms. Clear signage as you enter the park indicates the dangerous drop-offs and drowning risks, noting that some areas are one hundred feet deep. No lifeguards are on duty.

Before Travis County took charge of the park, it was privately owned and known as Windy Point. This name is not arbitrary; the wind does pick up here (making it a favorite destination for windsurfing). The water can be choppy, especially on days when the lake is busy with boat and Jet Ski traffic.

AMENITIES: Shaded picnic tables with grills. Boat ramp for nonmotorized craft. Restrooms with showers. Pavilion. Sand volleyball courts.

PRO TIP: Part of the charm of this park is its size, but the limited parking can mean visitors won't be admitted. It's wise to have a Lake Travis backup plan for the day. If you're up for a drive, check out Arkansas Bend Park for a similar beach experience.

Prince Solms Park

100 Liebscher Drive
New Braunfels, TX 78130
(830) 221-4350
nbtexas.org/1691/Prince-Solms-Park

HOURS: 10 a.m.–7 p.m.
ENTRANCE FEES: Free.
PARK RULES: City park rules apply.
CAMPING: Not available.
ABOUT: Prince Solms Park in New Braunfels, just down the street from Schlitterbahn New Braunfels Waterpark, is a

popular spot for family-friendly swimming and tubing. Prince Solms merges the natural beauty of the Comal River and dozens of close-set, moss-hung trees with the modern convenience of a concrete embankment, picnic areas, and the highly popular City Tube Chute. Plenty of paved walkways connect the various areas of the park, which is shaded by a variety of trees, including Texas persimmons, live oaks, pecans, and anaquas. A grassy slope rises above the concrete embankment, offering many picnic tables and grills. Above that are a golf course and playground. Across the way, private homes line the bank.

SWIMMING: The long, lazy waterway winds around a bend, where you can choose to drift or head for the Tube Chute. A series of wide steps arc into shallow water, offering easy access for young or timid swimmers.

AMENITIES: Restrooms. Drinking fountain. Nine-hole disc golf course. Tennis courts. Basketball courts. Tube Chute access.

PRO TIP: When searching for a place to park, steer clear of the Schlitterbahn crowds by staying on the south side of the river. Check out nearby downtown New Braunfels for a bite to eat or libations.

AUSTIN AREA

Rio Vista Park

Rio Vista Park
555 Cheatham Street
San Marcos, TX 78666
(512) 393-8400
ci.san-marcos.tx.us/

HOURS: 6 a.m.–11 p.m.

ENTRANCE FEES: Free.

PARK RULES: Styrofoam, glass, alcohol, public display and consumption of alcohol, smoking, and camping prohibited. Pets must be on leash.

CAMPING: Not available.

ABOUT: Full of tubers at the end of their ride down the river from San Marcos City Park, Rio Vista Dam at Rio Vista Park is a hotspot on the San Marcos River. Families set up grills, butterfly

chairs, and pop-up tents and play music to liven up a hot summer day. It's the pickup spot for Lions Club tube renters. (The starting point for the rental is in San Marcos City Park.) Close to main roads, this park has a definite city feel. Be prepared for a crowd on a hot summer weekend.

SWIMMING: The natural, rocky bank offers plenty of spots to step into the water. Two sets of short falls at Rio Vista make this a dynamic, attractive swim space. Children have fun riding the water over the falls, taking turns with kayakers and tubers who also enjoy the sweep of the water here. A stone embankment has been built as part of the tube rental and drop-off service; it's equipped with a ladder and stairs for easy entrance and exit. There is quite a bit of swim space here above the falls, though keep in mind that the water is shared with tubers and paddlers.

AMENITIES: Restrooms. Picnic tables with grills. Tennis courts. Basketball court. Hike and bike trails.

PRO TIP: If you find this spot too crowded, head across the street to William & Eleanor Crook Park, with its sweet little swimming holes on the San Marcos River.

AUSTIN AREA

River Trail Park

100 Paddling Trail Road
Luling, TX 78648
(830) 875-2481
cityofluling.net/facilities

HOURS: 7 a.m. to dusk.
ENTRANCE FEES: Free.
PARK RULES: Glass containers, open fires, firearms, and off-road vehicles prohibited.
CAMPING: Not available.
ABOUT: This simple, no-frills park on the San Marcos River

is a free, scenic place to relax and spread out for an afternoon. Conveniently located just off Route 90 on County Road 105 in Luling, this is a no-fuss spot where you can walk right into the pretty green waters of the San Marcos. Cottonwood trees offer a bit of shade, as does a picnic pavilion. There's plenty of green park space for picnicking. River Trail Park is the entry point for the Luling Zedler Mill Paddling Trail. Note that the roads in the park are unpaved. Vehicles park on the grass. The City of Luling does offer boat and kayak rentals here.

SWIMMING: A partially pebbled riverfront slopes directly into the water. You'll encounter some of the soft, silty bank found at other spots along the San Marcos. The bottom of the river is soft. Enjoy swimming in view of a small opposing cliff face, cottonwoods, and the active train trestle. No lifeguard is on duty; swim at your own risk.

AMENITIES: Picnic area. Pavilion.

PRO TIP: This is a great spot for families and water-loving dogs. The river bottom does drop off, so be sure young swimmers are wearing floatation devices.

AUSTIN AREA

Sandy Creek Park

9500 Lime Creek Road
Leander, TX 78641
parks.traviscountytx.gov/parks/sandy-creek

HOURS: Dawn to dusk.

ENTRANCE FEES: $10 per vehicle. $3 per pedestrian or cyclist. Free for seniors ages 62 and older and Lone Star veterans. Cash or check only; credit and debit cards not accepted. Camping fees apply.

PARK RULES: Public display or the consumption of alcoholic beverages or tobacco products, weapons, firearms, and fireworks prohibited. Pets must be on leash.

CAMPING: Primitive sites only on first come, first served basis. No reservations required. Quiet hours enforced from 10 p.m.–7 a.m.

ABOUT: Sandy Creek Park is a quiet, scenic spot located on a northern stretch of Lake Travis in the Texas Hill Country, a fair distance away from the bustling activity of the lake's southern shore. Its 25 acres include a unique wooded area ideal for nature walks, where you'll encounter a number of rare species of birds and plants, including the Golden-cheeked Warbler. Hiking along the bluff overlooking the water is a lovely way to take a break between swims.

SWIMMING: Water access is a short drive from the pay booth. Follow signs for the boat ramp, take the second left, and you'll find a small shady road where you can park your vehicle; there is no proper parking lot. From here, a short dirt trail cuts through trees down to the water. The rocky shoreline winds and turns, creating several nooks and crannies to settle down in this relatively quiet Lake Travis cove. Access to the water is from the medium-sized and large rocks that line the shore. There is no cover from the sun along the shore, so be sure to wear sun protection. The swimming area is roped off, which keeps

motorized boats at bay to an extent, though swimmers will feel the effects of the watercrafts' wakes, which can make the water quite choppy on a busy day. No lifeguard is on duty; swim at your own risk.

AMENITIES: Restrooms. Picnic areas with grills. Potable water. Primitive camping.

PRO TIP: Bring your water-loving dog to romp (on-leash) in the abundant space and easy water access here.

San Marcos City Park

216–298 City Park Street
San Marcos, TX 78666
(512) 393-8400
ci.san-marcos.tx.us

HOURS: 6 a.m.–11 p.m.

ENTRANCE FEES: Free.

PARK RULES: Styrofoam, alcohol, public display and consumption of alcohol, jumping or diving from bridges prohibited. Pets must be on leash.

CAMPING: Not available.

ABOUT: Located in the center of downtown San Marcos directly across the street from Texas State University, this 18-acre urban park is busy and much used by casual swimmers and tubers. In the summer months the Lions Club runs a bustling tube rental service out of the park's recreational hall. Rent a tube (or fill up your own with air), put it in at City Park, and float down the river for approximately an hour to Rio Vista Park, where the Lions Club bus will pick you up and drive you back to the rec center at City Park. Tube rental hours vary and are limited to Memorial Day through Labor Day.

SWIMMING: For casual swimmers, the river is accessible from either bank. Long steps have been carved out of the limestone on one side, offering space for sunbathing and stepping right down into the water. The bank on the other side of the river is grassy and slopes down under the shade of pecan trees. This is an easy place to take a break from the day and have a simple picnic. Beyond the swimming hole, a large field offers picnic tables and basketball courts.

AMENITIES: Restrooms with showers. Picnic area with grills. Potable water. Basketball courts. Hike and bike trails. Playground. Horseback riding.

PRO TIP: After your swim, take a stroll through nearby Spring Lake Natural Area, just over 250 acres of undeveloped park at the headwaters of the San Marcos River that's considered to be one of the oldest human-occupied areas in North America.

AUSTIN AREA

Sewell Park

601 University Drive
San Marcos, TX 78666
(512) 245-2004
campusrecreation.txstate.edu/outdoor/sewell-park.html

HOURS: 12 p.m.–6 p.m.

ENTRANCE FEES: Free.

PARK RULES: Styrofoam, alcohol, public display and consumption of alcohol, and jumping or diving from bridges prohibited. Pets must be on leash.

CAMPING: Not available.

ABOUT: Located on the campus of Texas State University but easily accessible to the public via city roads, Sewell Park has long been a place where students and San Marcos residents come to cool off in the crystal clear, spring-fed San Marcos River as it runs through the center of town. This is a great place to get a slice of San Marcos life and its locals.

Texas State opened the spot as Riverside Park in 1917 as a place for students to learn to swim. It was later renamed in honor of mathematics professor S. M. Sewell, who helped spur development of the park. Sewell Park sits alongside San Marcos City Park and includes many recreation activities, including volleyball courts, a basketball court, and plenty of places to enjoy a picnic. It's also the site of the annual commencement dive, when TSU graduates leap into the river in cap and gown.

SWIMMING: Access to the water is available from both banks of the river. Concrete steps lead down to the water on the west bank, which is closest to University Drive and the university. On the east bank a grassy lawn extends above a concrete path. From this side of the river, visitors have close access to the rest of the park and its activities and amenities. The blue-green San Marcos River keeps to a relatively cool 72° year round.

AMENITIES: Restrooms. Picnic areas with grills. Volleyball and basketball court.

PRO TIP: The San Marcos River is home to a native species of wild rice, the only plant that grows specifically in the river, which hosts several other endangered species as well. Protect this beautiful river and its natural resources. Tread delicately and take all trash when you go.

William & Eleanor Crook Park

430 Riverside Drive
San Marcos, TX 78666
(512) 393-8400
ci.san-marcos.tx.us

HOURS: 6 a.m.–11 p.m.
ENTRANCE FEES: Free.
PARK RULES: Styrofoam, alcohol, public display and consumption of alcohol, collection of firewood, nude sunbathing, and jumping or diving from bridges prohibited. Pets must be on leash.

CAMPING: Not available.

ABOUT: Across the street from bustling Rio Vista Park and its popular falls is a free, low-key, 6-acre city park where you can jump into the sparkling green San Marcos River as it winds its way through town. Once home to the San Marcos Nature Center, the park hosts a trailhead that provides access to hike and bike trails. Be sure to check out the vibrant mural painted on the side of the restroom facility in the parking lot. The artwork, by Mateo Jáimes, celebrates the city's unique natural environment. Parking is limited. For a simple swim that avoids the tube traffic, this is a great spot.

SWIMMING: A trail curves along the bank, where you'll find plenty of places to dive in, including a spot where a rope swing hangs above a good curve of the river. You'll feel as if you've discovered a series of secret swimming holes safe from the bustle of tubers and kayakers. No lifeguard is on duty; swim at your own risk.

AMENITIES: Restroom in the parking lot with a not-to-be-missed mural. Picnic tables with grills. Benches.

PRO TIP: Check out San Marcos Downtown Square, where you'll find plenty of shops, souvenirs, and other amenities.

AUSTIN AREA

Zedler Mill Park South

Texas Highway 80
Luling, TX 78648
(830) 875-5131
zedlermill.weebly.com/index

HOURS: 6 a.m.–11 p.m.

ENTRANCE FEES: Free.

PARK RULES: Styrofoam, alcohol, public display and consumption of alcohol, jumping or diving from bridges, collection of firewood, and nude sunbathing prohibited. Pets must be on leash.

CAMPING: Not available.

ABOUT: Across from historic Zedler Mill in quaint Luling is a peaceful spot to grab a swim in the pretty, jade waters of the San Marcos River. The turnoff to Zedler Mill Park South is just over the Texas 80 bridge, if you're heading south, and is marked by a Texas Paddling Trail sign on its gate. Follow an unpaved road down to the water, where you'll park on available grass. This is a no fuss, no muss, undeveloped spot. Ash, sycamore, and pecan trees offer shade along the banks.

A spacious park extends above the river. An unpaved trail winds a short way along the river, where the bank rises to a bluff frequented by visitors looking to fish. The south side of the park is a far more accessible route to the water than the mill side, where the bank is a bit high to comfortably get into the river.

SWIMMING: Step over the riverbank at just about any convenient point to access the water. The bank here is soft and muddy when wet, made of a fine clay that gives way under your feet when you step into the water. The river bottom is quite soft. For firmer ground beneath your feet as you get in, use the concrete boat ramp. It extends several feet into the water, and the river bottom around it is packed a little harder than along the bank.

The water gets deep fairly quick. Young swimmers should wear floaties to keep safe.

AMENITIES: Picnic areas with grills. Boat ramp.

PRO TIP: Zedler Mill is definitely worth checking out. The city revitalized the property and its 1870s buildings and turned the renovated mill into a museum and city park. The mill provides a great sense of the area's history and the important role the San Marcos River played in its economic development.

South

From Gonzales down to Lake Corpus Christi and over to Huntsville State Park, this small region (which doesn't include the coastal beaches) offers a variety of unique parks and swim spots. Choke Canyon is perhaps the most haunting of the lot, with its striking gold scrubland and earnest alligator warnings. For an extra dose of history, don't miss the portion of the Guadalupe River that runs through Gonzales, site of the famous "Come and Take It" Battle of Gonzales during the Texas Revolution. Families will want to make a beeline for Lake Corpus Christi State Park. And if you hit every spot and decide you still need another swim, shoot over to the Gulf islands and explore their many, many beaches.

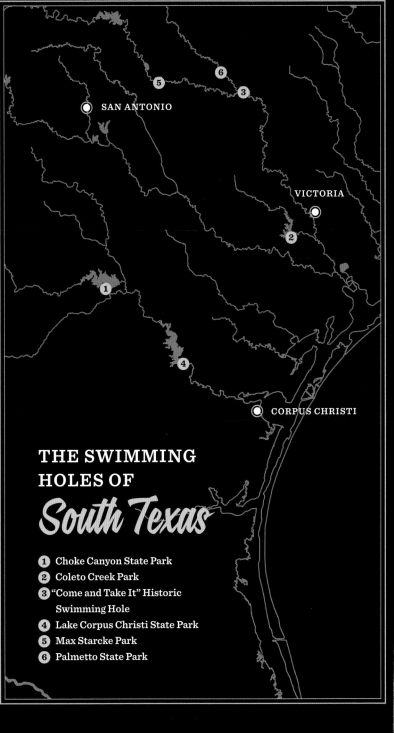

THE SWIMMING
HOLES OF
South Texas

1. Choke Canyon State Park
2. Coleto Creek Park
3. "Come and Take It" Historic
   Swimming Hole
4. Lake Corpus Christi State Park
5. Max Starcke Park
6. Palmetto State Park

Choke Canyon State Park

Calliham Unit
700 Texas 72
Three Rivers, TX 78071
(361) 786-3868
tpwd.texas.gov/state-parks/choke-canyon

HOURS: 6 a.m.–10 p.m.

ENTRANCE FEES: $5 per adult. Free ages 12 and under. Camping fees apply.

PARK RULES: Texas Parks & Wildlife rules apply.

CAMPING: Tent, RV (water and electric hookups), and shelters with air conditioning.

ABOUT: Down in South Texas, not far from the Gulf Coast, lies an isolated park rich with wildlife and golden brushland. Located just west of I-37 midway between San Antonio and Corpus Christi, the 26,000-acre Choke Canyon Reservoir at Choke Canyon State Park offers camping and recreation activities along its banks. The lake, marshlike at various points along the shoreline, is remarkable as the westernmost home of the American alligator. Dense mesquite and hackberry trees line the curving roads that take visitors between campgrounds to the large day-use area, where picnic tables dot a rolling hillside down to the water. Drive carefully and watch for deer, wild turkeys, javelinas, and many more creatures in the brush. The buzz of insects and caw of birds are the predominant sounds in this striking, memorable landscape.

Choke Canyon Reservoir, an impoundment of the Frio River, is a water source for Corpus Christi. The park's South Shore Unit is a day-use-only park that offers boating, picnicking, and wildlife viewing. The Calliham Unit offers the same activities, as well as camping.

SOUTH

SWIMMING: The swim experience at the Calliham Unit is neither for the faint of heart nor for novices to nature. While swimming is permitted anywhere along the shoreline of the reservoir, no specific swim area is designated due to the presence of alligators. All swimming is at your own risk. The rolling bank extends right into the still, murky water. Head down a trail worn into the brushland to reach the water's edge, and keep your eyes open for shore birds and any activity in the water. Swim shoes are recommended, as is keen attention to any other creatures who may be swimming in the water with you.

AMENITIES: Restrooms with showers. Picnic area with grills. Boat ramp. Volleyball courts. Softball area. Birding.

PRO TIP: Limited amenities are available outside the park. Bring what you need for the day. Be respectful of the wildlife that calls this beautiful park home.

Coleto Creek Park

365 Coleto Park Road
Victoria, TX 77905
(361) 575-6366
gbra.org/coletocreekpark

HOURS: 6 a.m.–midnight.
ENTRANCE FEES: $17 per vehicle per day. Maximum occupancy
per vehicle is four people. No day entry after 10 p.m. Individual
day use fee of $5 is charged for pedestrians, motorcyclists,
bicyclists, commercial bus passengers, and groups exceeding 4

people in 1 vehicle. $2 per pedestrian, cyclist, motorcycle, and per person for groups over four. Camping fees apply.

PARK RULES: Ground fires prohibited. All fires must be in fire ring/pits. Pets must be on leash. Other Guadalupe Basin River Authority rules outlined on the website.

CAMPING: Primitive, tent, and RV (water and electric hookups).

ABOUT: Managed by the Guadalupe Basin River Authority and Coleto Creek Power, Coleto Creek Park offers camping and recreational activities on the shores of 3,100-acre Coleto Creek Reservoir. A short drive southwest from Victoria and equidistant from Austin and Houston (each are 140 miles away), this park provides the only public access to the reservoir, which was created in 1980 as a cooling pond for the Coleto Creek Power coal plant. (Several similar lakes and reservoirs that serve the dual purpose of cooling pond and recreational area can be found in East Texas.) Coleto Creek Park is a popular family destination, heavily shaded and with ample space for picnicking and grilling.

SWIMMING: The designated swim area at Coleto is shallow, making it a great place for young swimmers. The deepest point, in the reservoir's center, reaches only twelve feet. Swimming is permitted anywhere along the shoreline. (Keep an eye out for submerged stumps and logs.) In the swim area, a grassy bank leads right into the water. Live oak trees grow quite close to the edge of the bank, providing an unusual amount of shade close to the water. The reservoir bottom here is firm and sandy. The water is warm in the summer months.

AMENITIES: Restrooms with showers. Picnic area with grills. Boat ramp. Playground. Hiking trails. Volleyball courts.

PRO TIP: Grab a dose of Texas history at nearby Goliad State Park and Historic Site on the San Antonio River, where you can visit places that figured prominently in the Texas Revolution.

SOUTH

"Come and Take It"
Historic Swimming Hole

**US Highway 183, beneath the Guadalupe River bridge
Gonzales, TX 78629**

HOURS: Natural, undeveloped swim spot. Swimming is dependent on weather and water levels.

ENTRANCE FEES: Free.

PARK RULES: Not part of a park system.

CAMPING: Not available.

ABOUT: Anyone who has studied Texas history knows well that Gonzales is more than just an average town in south Texas; it's the birthplace of Texas independence and the site of one of the most famous phrases uttered in Texas history: "Come and take it!" Modern-day Gonzales, south of I-10 between San Antonio and Houston, is festooned with flags commemorating the famous declaration of settlers who refused to turn a cannon over to Mexican soldiers. Visitors are welcome to cruise by two monuments installed on the site of the cannon confrontation—a place that happens to be just around the corner from the Guadalupe River, where you'll find a terrific spot to swim.

Head south on US 183 out of the center of town and watch for a sign pointing toward the historical markers. Hang a right, check out the monuments, then continue down the road around a small, grassy hill with picnic tables shaded by bald cypress and pecan trees. Here you'll discover a stretch of the Guadalupe that runs beneath the highway. The banks offer fairly easy access to the water for boaters and swimmers. This natural, completely undeveloped section of the Guadalupe, part of the Independence Paddling Trail, is popular with locals who want a casual place to listen to music, enjoy a few refreshing beverages, and take in the natural beauty of the river.

SWIMMING: The Guadalupe runs swift and crystal clear at this spot. Wade in at the bottom of the riverbank and be prepared for the current. Sit yourself down and hold on to the stones that line the riverbed or swim out further where the water deepens. Life jackets are recommended for young swimmers. For more adventure, head to a nearby bald cypress and grab the rope tied to one of its limbs. Swing out and drop into the refreshing river. Swim at your own risk.

AMENITIES: No amenities of any kind. Parking is ad hoc on the gravel and grass.

PRO TIP: Stop by the Gonzales Jail Museum in town where, in addition to touring the site, you can catch a tour of historic Gonzales.

SOUTH

Lake Corpus Christi State Park

23194 Park Road 25
Mathis, TX 78368
(361) 547-2635
tpwd.texas.gov/state-parks/lake-corpus-christi

HOURS: 7 a.m.–10 p.m.
ENTRANCE FEES: $5 per adult. Free ages 12 and under. Camping fees apply.
PARK RULES: Texas Parks & Wildlife rules apply.
CAMPING: Tent, RV (water and electric hookups), and screened shelters.

ABOUT: Located near the junction of I-37 and Texas Highway 359, this spacious park has a remarkably extensive shoreline and offers easy access to the warm, gentle waters of Lake Corpus Christi. It's an ideal place to relax, particularly for families with young children. The shoreline curves around a cove, winding in and out of several subtle nooks and crannies tucked beneath broad picnic areas. The slightly raised bank offers lovely views of the sparkling water and the activity around the cove. While there's plenty of space to spread out, shade is limited. The hardest part about visiting Lake Corpus Christi Park is picking just one beautiful spot to set up for the day.

Lake Corpus Christi is a 21,000-acre impoundment of the Nueces River. In 1934 the CCC (the same crew that moved on to build Palmetto State Park in 1936) carried out the unique vision of the park's architect to build a beautiful pavilion with stone arches, a stage, and a framed view of the lake, in addition to several other features. Take a moment to appreciate the work and the view.

SWIMMING: Swim access is available anywhere along the shore. In some places the grassy bank is higher than others, but no matter where you try to get in, you'll find it relatively easy to maneuver down to lake level and take a few flat, sandy steps right into the water. Some areas get deeper faster than others. The nook near the boat ramp between Opossum Bend Camping Loop and Bird's Nest Shelter Area is shallow, while the area in front of Mesquite Camping Area is mixed. Ask the park ranger at the visitors' center to point out the water's varying depths to suit your swim abilities.

AMENITIES: Restrooms with showers. Picnic areas with grills. Boat ramps. Fishing pier.

PRO TIP: Birders have long loved Lake Corpus Christi as a place to spot neotropical migrant birds. Binoculars up, y'all!

SOUTH

Max Starcke Park

115 South Austin Street
Seguin, TX 78155
(830) 401-2480
seguintexas.gov/departments/parks-and-recreations
/max-starcke-park.php

HOURS: M–F 6 a.m.–11 p.m., Sa–Su 6 a.m.–midnight.
ENTRANCE FEES: Free.
PARK RULES: In addition to posted rules, note that no alcohol is
allowed where children are at play.
CAMPING: Not available.
ABOUT: Max Starcke Park in Seguin offers many family-friendly
opportunities for fun outdoor activities along the Guadalupe
River. The park's 227 acres allow it to comfortably host a
multitude of activities and amenities. A golf course, volleyball
courts, walking trails, picnic tables, fishing spots, a playground,
a swimming hole and wave pool operated by the city, and more
make this a popular destination for families. Max Starcke also
offers access to the Seguin Paddling Trail.

The park was a project of the National Youth Administration,
which officially dedicated Max Starcke Park in 1938. Before
they began building, the property was a pecan orchard. The
Guadalupe's banks here remain thick with pecan trees and are

also studded with picnic tables and plenty of grassy spots to lay down a blanket.

SWIMMING: The section of river just above the Saffold Dam is easily accessible to swimmers. A set of curving steps wind down from the riverbank to a concrete outcropping perfect for launching yourself into the Guadalupe. A ladder drops down into the water there as well. The river is deep and calm here. The architecture of the steps and dock recall the park's late 1930s origins.

AMENITIES: Restrooms. Picnic areas with grills. Covered pavilions. Walking trails. Tennis, basketball, and volleyball courts. Playscape. Dog park. The park is also home to the Seguin Aquatic Center, where you'll find the wave pool open in the summer months.

PRO TIP: Grab a bite to eat at the old hydroelectric plant across the street, the Power Plant Texas Grill.

SOUTH

Palmetto State Park

78 Park Road 11 South
Gonzales, TX 78629
(830) 672-3266
tpwd.texas.gov/state-parks/palmetto

HOURS: Open 24/7. Gate is only locked for emergencies.
ENTRANCE FEES: $3 per adult. Free ages 12 and under. Camping fees apply.
PARK RULES: Texas Parks & Wildlife rules apply.
CAMPING: Tent, RV (water and electric hookups), and cabins.
ABOUT: Palmetto State Park in northwest Gonzales stands out

as one of the most unique parks in the Texas state park system. Here you'll find some of the state's finest examples of CCC work, a rich and varied natural swamp landscape, and if you keep your eyes open, you may possibly even come away with your own sighting of a North American wood ape, also known as "The Ottine Thing" (Texas's version of Bigfoot).

Palmetto lies in an area known as the Ottine Swamp, named for German settlers Adolph and Christine Otto. (Adolph combined their names to form Ottine. "He was a romantic fellow," according to a park ranger.) Several sulfur springs in the area combine with overflow from the San Marcos River, which by the time it reaches Palmetto has merged with the Blanco River.

The CCC is responsible for several of the structures and features in the park, including the refectory, the water tower, concrete picnic tables, and more. Five miles of hiking trails wind through trees that shade a rich understory consisting of a wide variety of plants, including the dwarf palmetto that gives the park its name.

SWIMMING: Palmetto offers two swim spots. The most direct is spring-fed Oxbow Lake. This picturesque, grass-lined lake is visible from the bridge as you enter the park. Walk-in access is available from its banks. A swim platform floats out in the water, which does get deep. Bald cypress and oak trees grow right up to the edge of the lake and offer a fair amount of shade. This spot is near a campsite, so day users will share the space and the water with campers. Deeper within the park, the San Marcos River is also accessible at a low-water crossing down a trail near the refectory.

AMENITIES: Restrooms with showers. Hiking trails. Picnic areas with grills. Boat ramp. Park store.

PRO TIP: Before you leave, make sure you take a drive up Park Road 11 and veer left at the fork into Ottine. The scenic overlook—and the tree-lined road leading up to it—will make you fall in love with Texas all over again.

West

Mythic, mysterious, miraculous West Texas: land of Big Bend, big skies, desert storms, and no cell phone service. In this book, West Texas starts at Del Rio and includes the area south of Interstate 10, sticking relatively close to the border with Mexico. The swim spots out here are far between, but it's well worth the miles covered to find them. There's no promise that the Chihuahuan Desert will save your soul, but it will certainly set you to thinking about the vast stars above and the enormous earth beneath your feet. And it will definitely make you ready to swim. With temperatures that can make a rock sweat, the places that exist out here to cool off and refresh are vital. From downtown Del Rio to the foothills of the Davis Mountains (where your soul really will be saved by San Solomon Springs at Balmorhea), there is nothing like going for a swim—in springwater or among the stars—in West Texas.

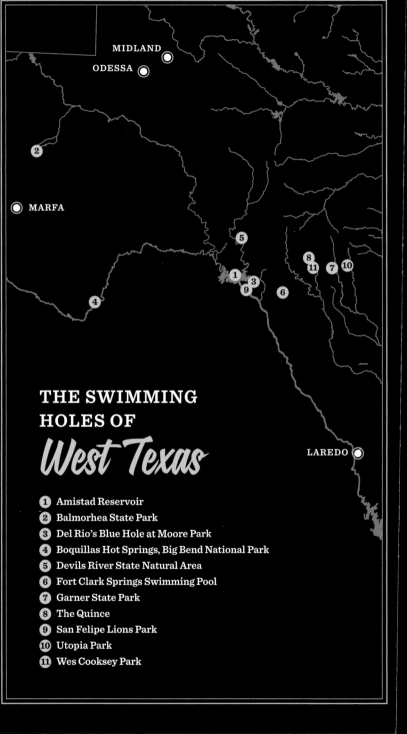

THE SWIMMING
HOLES OF
West Texas

1. Amistad Reservoir
2. Balmorhea State Park
3. Del Rio's Blue Hole at Moore Park
4. Boquillas Hot Springs, Big Bend National Park
5. Devils River State Natural Area
6. Fort Clark Springs Swimming Pool
7. Garner State Park
8. The Quince
9. San Felipe Lions Park
10. Utopia Park
11. Wes Cooksey Park

MIDLAND

ODESSA

MARFA

LAREDO

Amistad Reservoir

Amistad National Recreation Area
9685 US Highway 90 West
Del Rio, TX 78840
(830) 775-7491
nps.gov/amis/index.htm

HOURS: Open 24/7. Visitors' center open 8 a.m.–4:30 p.m.
ENTRANCE FEES: Free. Camping fees apply.
PARK RULES: National Park rules apply. Obey all posted signs.
CAMPING: Five designated campgrounds offer sites on first come, first served basis. Tent and RV (no hookups). Three group campsites available by reservation. Call in advance to reserve.
ABOUT: Lake Amistad (or Amistad Reservoir) is a breathtaking, oceanic sweep of blue-grey that straddles the border between

WEST

the United States and Mexico at Del Rio. The lake covers 89,000 acres on both sides of the border; two-thirds of the reservoir lies on the US side. The national park's recreational area covers 58,500 total acres, opening up the desert landscape and its rocky bluffs to visitors via several entrance points off US Highway 90. Day-use areas include Governors Landing, Diablo East, eight picnic areas, and various overlooks.

Lake Amistad and the Amistad Dam are owned and managed by the United States and Mexico through the International Boundary and Water Commission. They are the result of a partnership between the two countries struck in the 1960s to manage flooding and harness the power of the Rio Grande for hydroelectricity and irrigation. Amistad means "friendship" in Spanish.

SWIMMING: Lake Amistad has two designated, unsupervised swim areas: Governors Landing and Diablo East. Many entrance signs for Amistad Recreational Area appear along US 90. Look for signs that specifically say "Governors Landing" or "Diablo East." The terrain at both spots is rocky; wear swim shoes. Also bring at least a gallon of drinking water per person.

Governors Landing is the more accessible of the two swim areas. Turn off 90 onto a paved road that takes you to a small parking lot at the top of a rocky hill. A picnic area with covered tables offers tremendous views of the water. Restrooms are available as well. A gravel trail to the left of the parking lot leads down to the lake. The rocky shoreline curves in and out as it slopes gently into the water, where you can swim beneath the US 90 bridge and in view of an old train trestle. The bottom is rocky. The water gets deep fairly quickly and stretches out far beyond the bridge and trestle. Water temperatures range from the mid-50s to the mid-80s, depending on the time of year. Between the vast, flat lake and the endless sky, this is an otherworldly spot to float, sandwiched between natural blues.

Diablo East offers a spectacular view, though swim access is limited. Turn off US 90 and head down Viewpoint Road.

If you reach the parking lot for the marina, you've gone too far. Look for signs that point toward the dive cove and swimming area. You'll have to park where there's space at the end of the dirt-and-gravel road. The swim area is off a floating dock at the bottom of a steep, rocky cliff. A concrete path runs down the length of the cliff to the dock. While this makes the trip somewhat easier to traverse, the incline is still quite steep and should be descended with care. Jump off the dock into the water and enjoy the phenomenal views of the cove. Neither spot has a lifeguard; swim at your own risk.

AMENITIES: Covered picnic tables. Restrooms. Big Bend Natural History Association bookstore, located in the visitors' center, which also offers a small inventory of items for sale, movies about the region visitors can borrow, exhibits, and information about the park and other nearby sites.

PRO TIP: The long human history in this area dates back to the Ice Age. Several nearby caves are home to four-thousand-year-old rock art. While the reservoir has submerged many of these caves, some are accessible and the art visible. Boat tours are available out of Amistad to Panther and Parida Caves, where you can view examples of the art. Nearby Seminole Canyon State Park and Historic Site and Galloway White Shaman Preserve offer guided tours.

WEST

Balmorhea State Park

9207 Texas Highway 17 South
Toyahvale, TX 79786
(432) 375-2370
tpwd.texas.gov/state-parks/balmorhea

HOURS: 8 a.m.–7:30 p.m. (or dusk, whichever comes first).
ENTRANCE FEES: $7 per adult. Free ages 12 and under.
PARK RULES: Texas Parks & Wildlife rules apply.
CAMPING: Tent and RV (water and electric hookups). Rooms available for rent on-site at San Solomon Springs Courts.
ABOUT: Out in the far reaches of the West Texas desert, in the

foothills of the Davis Mountains, a veritable oasis bubbles up from the ground: San Solomon Springs in Balmorhea State Park. Just a few miles south of I-10 and about an hour west of Fort Stockton, this spring-fed swimming pool, the largest in the world, holds 3.5 million gallons of clear, clean water from the San Solomon Springs and draws thousands of people each year to swim, sunbathe, and camp in this remote locale.

Developing Balmorhea State Park was a major project for the CCC. From 1936 to 1941 thousands of men lived at the site, sleeping in barracks and eating at a mess hall they built themselves. They built the V-shaped 1.75 acre pool, the bathhouse, a concession building, San Solomon Springs Courts, and other features. Low and unobtrusive, the CCC's architecture blends with the natural surroundings. Please note that in recent years, the park has been subject to frequent closures, both scheduled and unexpected, in order to improve the pool and grounds. Be sure to check with Texas State Parks about Balmorhea's status before making the trip.

SWIMMING: In the center of the pool, twenty-five feet underwater, San Solomon Springs pours out fifteen million gallons of crystal-blue, $72-75°$ water every day. A concrete embankment runs around the diameter of the pool and offers several easy access points via metal ladders, concrete steps, and a wheelchair lift. The enormous pool of pristine springwater coupled with the vast view of mountains in the distance makes Balmorhea an unforgettable swim experience and well worth the drive to get here.

AMENITIES: Restrooms. Picnic tables with grills. Playground. Diving board.

PRO TIP: Visit the park's two reconstructed *cienega*s (wetlands), whose waters are home to several species of fish, including two endangered species, the Comanche Springs pupfish and the Pecos gambusia, as well as turtles who emerge to sun themselves. Watch for the many cottontails that hop out from the brushland around campsites at dusk and dawn.

WEST

Del Rio's Blue Hole at Moore Park

US Highway 90 East, along San Felipe Creek
Del Rio, TX 78840
cityofdelrio.com

HOURS: 6 a.m.–10 p.m.

ENTRANCE FEES: Free.

PARK RULES: City park rules apply. Glass containers and littering prohibited. No bicycles, motorcycles, or horses. Dogs permitted in the water but must be on leash.

CAMPING: Not available.

ABOUT: Known to locals as the Blue Hole, this natural swim spot sits on a stretch of San Felipe Creek that runs along the northwest edge of Moore Park, right off busy Highway 90 in Del Rio. You may not find this spot marked on a map as "Blue Hole." Searching online, you're more likely to find reference to the Moore Park Pool, a chlorinated pool located deeper in the park. To locate the Blue Hole, find Moore Park and watch for the parking lot off Highway 90. When you see a train trestle and a smaller bridge, you'll know you've found the spot.

This city park is conveniently located in central Del Rio. The creek is fed by San Felipe Springs, the westernmost group of springs discharged by the Edwards Aquifer. The impounding of Lake Amistad in the late 1960s increased the flow of these artesian springs, keeping the creek at a reliable level. Walk the paved path along the creek up from Blue Hole into Moore Park and you'll find covered picnic tables, basketball courts, a base-ball park, and a view of the back of Moore Park Pool. Long used by the military as a campsite, this area was originally an outpost of Fort Clark and was also a campsite for the experimental US Army Camel Corps in the late 1850s.

SWIMMING: The springwater here is cold and clear, rushing over an elevated rock shelf to form a very short falls. The creek, which is mostly shallow, is accessible via natural outcroppings of limestone that step down into the water. This picturesque spot is framed by a working train trestle to the south and a small concrete pedestrian bridge to the north. The long rock shelf above the falls provides a calm (if slippery) place to lounge and wade, while the active area below the falls offers a deeper pocket of water and the fun of crashing water. A grassy, well-maintained area studded with trees offers limited but vital shade along the western bank. No lifeguard is on duty; swim at your own risk. Keep in mind that this spot is highly popular with locals. Expect to share space.

AMENITIES: Restrooms, picnic tables with grills, and athletic facilities available within Moore Park.

PRO TIP: Hang out long enough for a train to pass overhead while you swim. Afterwards, check out Val Verde Winery, the oldest continuously running winery in Texas. They make olive oil, too!

Boquillas Hot Springs, Big Bend National Park

PO Box 129
Big Bend National Park, TX 79834
(432) 477-2251
nps.gov/bibe/planyourvisit/soakinthesprings.htm

HOURS: Park entrances open 24/7. Hours vary for fee stations and visitors' centers.

ENTRANCE FEES: $30 per vehicle.

PARK RULES: (Specific to Boquillas Springs) Soak only. Do not use soaps or oils. Keep the area clean and remove trash. Alcoholic beverages, glass containers, and overnight camping prohibited.

CAMPING: Primitive, tent, and RV (water and electric hookups) elsewhere in the park.

ABOUT: A short, popular hike in Big Bend National Park, the

WEST

Boquillas Hot Springs offer an opportunity to submerge in natural heated water in a rugged environment and to discover a unique piece of Texas history.

The springs have drawn life for thousands of years. Evidence of an ancient bathtub dug out of stone, Native American pictographs above the springs, and tales of the Comanche Trail indicate a long human history here. The springs gained widespread notoriety in the early 1900s when J. O. Langford sought them out on rumor of the restorative powers of their mineral salts. Quickly convinced of the water's efficacy, he built a bathhouse and began to advertise in the *Alpine Avalanche* newspaper. Langford's structures, though crumbling, remain at Boquillas as the Hot Springs Historic District, as does the bathing basin Langford built around the springs. The springs are a short half-mile hike from the Hot Springs parking lot. There is a fair amount of shade at the entrance to the trail, but the trail itself is unshaded. The hike is rocky and uneven and runs alongside a high limestone cliff. Wear good hiking shoes.

SWIMMING: This is a spot for soaking rather than swimming. While the Rio Grande runs right beside the springs, high bacteria counts and unpredictable currents in the river make for an unsafe swim environment, so stay within the spring's stone basin. Also be mindful of whether the river has recently swollen and covered the springs. The springs themselves are a consistent 105°, heated by geothermal processes on their way to the surface. Sit in the warm, mineral-rich water and enjoy the same healing powers humans have been seeking here for centuries.

AMENITIES: Restrooms near the parking lot.

PRO TIP: Bring water. Lots of it. And make sure to spend plenty of time in the rest of the park. Stick around and camp. Big Bend is a destination.

Devils River State Natural Area

HC 01
PO Box 513
Del Rio, TX 78840
(830) 395-2133
tpwd.texas.gov/state-parks/devils-river

HOURS: F–M 8 a.m.–5 p.m., Tu–Th closed.

ENTRANCE FEES: Free.

PARK RULES: Texas Parks & Wildlife rules apply. No trash service. Pack it in. Pack it out.

CAMPING: Tent camping only, by reservation only, made at least one day in advance. Call (512) 389-8901 for information, availability, and fees.

ABOUT: Located at the nexus of the Chihuahuan Desert (to the west), the Tamaulipan region (to the south and east), and the Edwards Plateau and the Hill Country (to the north), the 37,000-acre Devils River Natural Area is a biodiverse region home to unique plant and animal life. Waters from several springs merge here to form Devils River, one of the most unspoiled, intact rivers in Texas. Devils River flows through primitive wilderness and is mostly inaccessible over its course from the headwaters to Lake Amistad, where it empties. The natural area open to the public offers few amenities: a restroom and shower are available near park headquarters, and a restroom is available near the swim spot, San Pedro Park. In between you'll encounter nothing but desert. Paddling is the most popular activity on Devils River, though even experienced paddlers are cautioned about the river's rapids and few points of portage.

Visiting the river requires a one-and-a-half to two-hour drive into the desert from Del Rio, followed by a mile-long hike.

Gas up before you head in and bring plenty of water and food. To access the entrance, turn off State Highway 277 onto Dolan Road, a gravel-and-dirt road that winds through private ranchland for twenty-two miles before reaching the natural area's main entrance. As the desert cliffs and hills open up around you, be aware of roadrunners, rabbits, and other native life that may cross your path, including grazing cattle. Low-water crossings appear regularly. While this road is relatively easy to traverse, be sure your tank is topped up and your tires are in excellent shape, as there are no gas or service stations for at least twenty-five miles after that Dolan Road turnoff. Once you're off the highway, there's nothing but private land, homes, and desert.

SWIMMING: Swimming in Devils River is a commitment. Part of what has maintained the river's beauty and pristine ecology is its limited accessibility. From the natural area's entrance, follow posted directional signs that say, simply, "River." The road leading deeper into the natural area is narrow, rocky, and subject to sharp inclines and declines. If you're driving a car with low clearance, take extreme care. Vehicles with raised chassis and good tires are recommended. Be mindful of oncoming traffic, as the road is narrow. While this is a remote area, visitors do come to fish and swim.

The trail from the parking area down to the river must be taken on foot. (Wear sturdy walking shoes or hiking boots.) Also rocky and uneven, the trail winds through breathtaking cliffs and desert vegetation buzzing with birds, insects, and wildlife. There is no shade, so sun protection is vital. This can be a strenuous walk for inexperienced hikers, particularly in and around the summer months. Pack light and bring more water than you think you'll need. Eventually you'll crest an incline that offers a glimpse of the river's surface, a welcome relief on a hot day.

Devils River has several incarnations along its course, from serene pools to violent rapids and treacherous waterfalls. At San Pedro Point the water is relatively still and shallow. Pockets of life shoot up from the riverbed while schools of small fish dart beneath the surface in search of food. Step into the water through a clearing in the brush. The bottom of the river is lined with smooth, slippery stones. Swim shoes are recommended. This is a literal oasis in the desert, a trip into remarkable and unforgettable territory.

AMENITIES: Restrooms. Shower.

PRO TIP: Water, water, water, water, water—bring drinking water. Sun protection is vital, as is overall preparation for the trip. Keep in mind that you will not have GPS or cell service.

WEST

Fort Clark Springs Swimming Pool

300 US Highway 90
Brackettville, TX 78832
(830) 563-2493
fortclark.com

HOURS: Open to the public on some holidays; call to confirm.

ENTRANCE FEES: $3 per person. Members and guests must register and receive a tag from on-site attendant. Camping fees apply.

PARK RULES: RVs, ATVs, horses, dogs off-leash, glass containers, profanity, and loud music prohibited in swim areas. Swimmers must wear appropriate swimwear in the water.

CAMPING: Tent and RV (water and electric hookups).

ABOUT: Fort Clark Springs is a 2,700-acre gated resort and leisure community approximately 125 miles west of San Antonio. Its residents preserve local history while welcoming visitors to enjoy the impressive man-made pool built around Las Moras Springs. Long a campground for Native American tribes— including the Comanches, who made this a stop on their war trail to Mexico—the site of Las Moras Springs was used as a US military fort for mounted cavalry from 1852 until World War II. Many of the original barracks and other fort buildings remain. The fort and its buildings are listed on the National Register of Historic Places. Pick up a map at the booth on your way in and take a walking tour of the Fort Clark Historic District, which includes the blacksmith shop, antebellum log officers' quarters, and a theater.

SWIMMING: The pool at Fort Clark Springs is stunning. Clear, blue-green water from Las Moras Springs fills an enormous three-hundred-foot man-made pool, one of the largest in Texas, which varies in depth from just under three feet at its shallow end to over eight and a half feet at its deep end. A short wall sections off a portion of the shallow end from the rest of the pool, so there's no worry that your young or inexperienced swimmers might drift above their heads. The springwater is a cool 68° year round.

Las Moras Springs releases more than twelve million gallons of water daily. Lifeguards are on duty from 1 p.m. to 9 p.m. Before then, swim at your own risk. A concrete embankment rims the pool, and ladders descend into the water; a long walkway slopes into the water near the shallow end. While the swimming area itself is unshaded, the verdant park encircling the pool offers ample shade from ash, magnolia, pecan, bald cypress, and live oak trees. Picnic areas abound.

AMENITIES: Restrooms with showers. Picnic tables with grills. Playground. Concession stand.

PRO TIP: Check out nearby Kickapoo Cavern State Park to explore numerous caves and see the Mexican free-tailed bats emerge at dusk.

Garner State Park

234 RR 1050
Concan, TX 78838
(830) 232-6132
tpwd.texas.gov/state-parks/garner

HOURS: 8 a.m.–10 p.m.

ENTRANCE FEES: $8 per adult. Free ages 12 and under. Camping fees apply.

PARK RULES: Texas Parks & Wildlife rules apply.

CAMPING: Tent, RV (water and electric hookups), screened shelters, and cabins.

ABOUT: At the southwestern edge of the Texas Hill Country sits Concan, a small town that serves as a gateway to the Frio River. Here you'll find a culture that caters to river tourism; several

shops sell swimwear, sunglasses, inflatable floats, noodles, sun hats, souvenirs, picnic supplies, and various other accessories for making the most of a day spent tubing on the Frio.

The primary public swim spot in Concan, Garner State Park, is located a short drive north of town on US Highway 83. Established in 1941 as a project of the CCC, this park is famed not only for its prime swimming and overnight camping, but also for dancing at its CCC-built pavilion. In the spring and summer months, locals and visitors line dance and two-step to country and western standards every night. The family-friendly affair has become a beloved local tradition. Add Garner to your bucket list of state parks to visit—it's a highly social, busy, beautiful spot to dip in and to get to know folks who also like to relax and revel in the state's impressive natural landscape.

SWIMMING: Swimming at Garner State Park is incredibly popular. The eastern edge of the park is bounded by nearly three miles of the clear, green Frio River, and you'll have easy access from the day-use area for swimming, floating, and tubing. This site (within easy driving distance of both Austin and San Antonio) limits the number of people allowed in the park, and maximum capacity can be reached as early as 10 a.m. during peak swim season, so be sure to arrive early and have an alternative plan ready in case the park is full by the time you get there. (Nearby Mager's Crossing might be an option.) Bald cypress roots grow into the water along the edge of the riverbank; to the right, an impressive limestone cliff frames the scenery. The view here is both serene and breathtaking, and it's a large reason why Garner attracts so many visitors. It can and does get crowded here. No lifeguard is on duty; swim at your own risk.

AMENITIES: Restrooms with showers. Picnic tables with grills. Hiking trails. Park store.

PRO TIP: Book ahead! The popularity of this park cannot be overstated. Plan your trip around a night when there's a band performing at the dancehall.

WEST

The Quince

River Road, off Texas Route 55
Camp Wood, TX 78833

HOURS: Natural, undeveloped swim spot. Swimming is dependent on weather and water levels.
ENTRANCE FEES: Free.
PARK RULES: Not part of a park system.
CAMPING: Not available.
ABOUT: Known as "the swim spot" to locals, this natural, undeveloped pocket of the Nueces River north of Uvalde in the small town of Camp Wood is a picturesque spot to jump in. Take Route 55 to River Road; less than a quarter mile in, you'll hit the Quince. This spot is entirely unshaded, so plan on bringing plenty of sun protection. This is an all natural swim experience. No restrooms or potable water are available, so be sure to bring plenty of drinking water.
SWIMMING: The sparkling, blue-green water of the Nueces cuts through low, limestone bluffs. A short climb down a rocky bank puts you in the water. The water depth reaches approximately fifteen feet, giving the spot its name. ("Quince" means "fifteen" in Spanish.) The Nueces is narrow here, and you can easily swim from one side to the other. A small pebble shore offers a place to sit on the far bank.
AMENITIES: No amenities of any kind. Park along the side of the road. Take care entering and exiting your vehicle.
PRO TIP: This is an easy spot to bring your water-loving dog. Just be sure to also bring plenty of water and your own shade.

WEST

San Felipe Lions Park

De La Rosa Street and Gillis Street
Del Rio, TX 78840
cityofdelrio.com

HOURS: 6 a.m.–10 p.m.

ENTRANCE FEES: Free.

PARK RULES: City park rules apply. Dogs permitted in the water but must be on leash. No bicycles, motorcycles, horses, or glass containers. No littering. City rules regarding alcohol consumption apply.

CAMPING: Not available.

ABOUT: San Felipe Lions Park is a spacious, sparkling gem in southeast Del Rio. This clean, well-maintained park at the intersection of De La Rosa and Gillis Streets offers plenty of comfortable access to San Felipe Creek and makes for a great opportunity to float in a tube. It's part of the San Felipe Creek Walk, so a concrete path runs alongside the water. Besides swimming, you'll find plenty of picnic tables, playground equipment, and a basketball court to keep yourself occupied. The park is also the site of Tardy Dam, built in the late 1800s, which creates a small falls. In 1976 the Lions Club took over management of the park from the city and gave it its current name. The Lions added a stone entrance and enhanced other amenities. This is a lovely, developed park that has managed to maintain its impressive natural beauty.

SWIMMING: From the concrete embankment, swimmers can get in just about anywhere along the creek, though be aware that the water is deep. A half-moon of concrete steps descend into the water near the center of the park. The steps end at a wide concrete shelf with a lip, where the water is shallow and good for little swimmers. The other popular swim spot is on the other side of the short wall of Tardy Dam. Here, natural rock

formations create comfortable spots to sit, soak, and swim while the water rushes over the dam falls. For extra fun, look for the rope swing. No lifeguard is on duty; swim at your own risk.

AMENITIES: Restrooms. Picnic tables with grills. Playground.

PRO TIP: This is a top pick for all of Texas, especially for families. The San Felipe Creek Walk runs through this park. Be sure to take a stroll north on the Creek Walk and check out the vibrant murals beneath the nearby low bridge.

WEST

Utopia Park

241 Utopia Park Road
Utopia, TX 78884
(830) 966-3643
utopiapark.org

HOURS: Dawn to dusk for motorized vehicles.

ENTRANCE FEES: $10 per day per person.

PARK RULES: Glass containers prohibited. Pets must be on leash.

CAMPING: Tent, RV (water and electric hookups), and screened shelters.

ABOUT: For a dose of small-town Texas and a respite from the crowds on the Frio River, head southeast of Leakey (pronounced LAKE-ee) to Utopia, a town with no red lights that boasts one of the most beautiful hidden gems in the Uvalde County area, Utopia Community Park. Drive past the old baseball field and into a picturesque grove of cypresses alongside a perfect little piece of Sabinal River. Their magical canopy offers a secluded place to relax and get in the water. Plenty of picnic tables and grills are available for use.

SWIMMING: This small, quiet spot offers tons of shade, a rope swing, and good swimming up above the dam. The cool, crystal-clear Sabinal isn't too wide here, offering plenty of space to swim out and float, and for strong swimmers, the fun of swimming shore to shore. The river bottom is soft and spotted with rocks. Some vegetation grows on the bottom, particularly close to shore; swim shoes are a good idea. No lifeguard is on duty; swim at your own risk.

AMENITIES: Restrooms with showers. Picnic tables with grills.

PRO TIP: This is a good place to stop for a spell if you're headed farther north on Texas Highway 187 to hike at Lost Maples State Natural Area. For a deeper look into the town of Utopia and the lives of its residents, pick up a copy of Karen Valby's *Welcome to Utopia: Notes from a Small Town.*

Wes Cooksey Park

33719 Texas Route 55
Camp Wood, TX 78833
(830) 597-3223

HOURS: 8 a.m.–9 p.m.

ENTRANCE FEES: $4 per person.

PARK RULES: Alcohol and glass prohibited. No pets in the swim area.

CAMPING: Tent and RV (water and electric hookups). Waterfront sites available.

ABOUT: If you really want to get away from the crowded river culture in Uvalde, head beyond the Frio and Sabinal Rivers toward the town of Camp Wood, where you'll find quiet access to spring-fed Nueces Lake at Wes Cooksey Park.

Three miles south of town, this well-tended spot hosts thirty tent and RV sites right on the bank of an impounded portion

of the Nueces. The water here is deep, and the park's a popular spot for both swimming and fishing. The tent sites are cozy and somewhat private; each site is marked off by natural landscaping. Day users pay a small per-person fee and are assigned their own site. Stop at the office at the front entrance, where you can pay the fee.

SWIMMING: A shallow wood dock just to the right of the dam wall provides a spot to sit and dangle your feet in the cold water. Plenty of fish swim below the surface, including catfish, bass, and perch. A metal ladder beside the narrow dock steps down into the water. Young swimmers should be closely supervised and given proper floatation devices to keep safe in the deep water. The view here is tremendous, with high Texas hills rising above the calm, mirrorlike lake.

AMENITIES: Restrooms with showers. Picnic tables with grills.

PRO TIP: Come here and never leave. The park can be busy, and campsites are limited. If you plan to camp on a summer weekend, be sure to call ahead before driving out.

Top Five Lists

BEST SPOTS FOR ACCESSIBILITY

These spots offer a natural swim experience outfitted with paved walkways, shallow ends, and concrete embankments surrounding the water.

TOP FIVE FREE SPOTS

TOP FIVE SPOTS FOR KIDS

TOP FIVE DOG-FRIENDLY SPOTS

TOP FIVE FOR CAMPING

TOP FIVE WORTH THE DRIVE

TOP FIVE OFF THE BEATEN PATH

TOP FIVE PLACES WE MUST PROTECT

Acknowledgments

Thank you, first and foremost, to Brian Contine, for having the brilliant idea to make this book. Thank you to Casey Kittrell and University of Texas Press for supporting this book and making it the best it can be. Major thanks to Douglas Shuga and Christopher Courville for their work editing, swimming, and feeding the animals while we were on the road.

Deep gratitude and respect to all of the park rangers and employees whose love for these beautiful places protects them and makes them accessible to all of us.